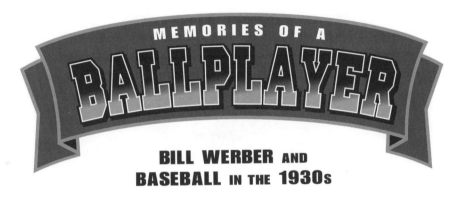

MEMORIES OF A BALLPLAYER

BILL WERBER AND BASEBALL IN THE 1930s

Bill Werber and
C. Paul Rogers III

Published by The Society for American Baseball Research (SABR)
812 Huron Road, Suite 719, Cleveland, OH 44115
www.sabr.org

Distributed by the University of Nebraska Press
233 North 8th Street, Lincoln, NE 68588-0255
www.nebraskapress.unl.edu

Cover design by Ronnie Joyner

Photo Credits: National Baseball Hall of Fame, George Brace, Transcendental Graphics,
Cincinnati *Post*, Bill Werber, C. Paul Rogers III

Printed and manufactured by EBSCO Media, Birmingham, Alabama

Earlier versions of chapter 2 and chapter 13 were published in
Elysian Fields Quarterly, Nine: A Journal of Baseball History and
Social Policy Perspective, respectively.

To Kathryn Potter Werber who blessed me with a wonderful marriage for over 70 years. We met on the opening day of school at Tech High in Washington, D.C. in September of 1924 and were married on September 16, 1929 before my senior year at Duke University. Tat was the inspiration that prompted me to do well scholastically and to excel athletically and hers was the leveling influence that guided the lives of our children. All honor to her name.

Bill Werber

To my mother, Leigh Galloway Rogers, a wonderful woman who doesn't watch much baseball but who is always there when the chips are down.

Paul Rogers

TABLE OF CONTENTS

1 WITH THE `27 YANKEES AND BREAKING INTO PROFESSIONAL BASEBALL

I am probably the last person alive to have a direct connection with the 1927 Yankees, arguably the best baseball club of all time. That team won 110 ball games, won the American League pennant by a mere nineteen games, and swept four straight from the Pittsburgh Pirates in the World Series. Dubbed "Murderers Row" by the sportswriters, they were a group of raucous, swashbuckling, carefree winners who hit often and for distance and had a good time while at it. These big, tough, rugged guys were managed by a mite of an intellectual named Miller Huggins. I was, for a while, sort of a member of that ball club.

The 1927 Duke freshman baseball team was, in its class, equivalent to the Yankees, with all four infielders hitting in the .365 to .450 range. Scouts from the big leagues were often in the stands—Doyle from Detroit, Rapp from Cleveland, Devlin from the Giants, Molesworth from the Pirates, Rickey from the Cardinals, and the legendary Paul Krichell from the Yankees. Our coach, George "Possum" Whitted, had been a National League outfielder for eleven years, and I often wondered exactly what part he played in the appearance of these scouts and whether he was compensated for his efforts when his players signed.

Krichell, best known for finding and signing Lou Gehrig, was above the cut, well-mannered, articulate, and forceful in selling the advantages of playing with Babe Ruth in Yankee Stadium. That spring, near the end of my freshman year, Krichell made an offer: a cash down payment, the cost of my next three years at Duke, a bonus upon graduation, and the signing of a Yankee contract and a set monthly salary when I reported. The deal was struck with a handshake and a meeting of the eyes between Krichell and my father. Both parties kept the agreement. Technically, I received no money. Factually, I did. Krichell called upon my dad in Washington, D.C., and deposited the agreed-upon sums with him. It amounted to something in the vicinity of $12,000 and relieved my dad of the financial hardship of the rest of my education. After we shook hands on this arrangement, Mr. Krichell suggested that I travel with the Yankees that summer to further my baseball education. He had high respect for Miller Huggins, the Yankee manager, and thought I could learn a lot just by sitting next to him on the bench and rubbing elbows with the likes of Ruth and Gehrig. The Yankees agreed to pay me $350 a month, which was more money than I had ever seen.

I was apprehensive about going to New York. Frankly, the city intimidated me. I was nineteen years old and the farthest I had been from my small hometown of Berwyn, Maryland, was Durham, North Carolina, to attend Duke. When I arrived in New York I reported to Ed Barrow, the Yankee general manager, at his office near 42nd and Broadway. He directed me to the Colonial Hotel, which was not impressive. The only other Yankee staying there was Charley O'Leary, a coach. I cannot remember eating with him or speaking to him at the hotel, although he was the only member of the club who paid any attention to me at the stadium. I was pretty lonely. I ate by myself, lived alone, and traveled to and from the ballpark on the subway with the other denizens of the city.

It was no better at the ballpark. This was a hard-nosed, tobacco-chewing crew—guys like Ruth, Gehrig, Lazzeri, Combs, Meusel, Koenig, Dugan, Grabowski, and Collins—and they had neither the time nor the inclination to extend any courtesies to me. If I got out to shortstop during batting practice to take a few grounders, infielders like Mark Koenig or Mike Gazella would yell, "Get out of here, kid." The same thing would happen if

I went to the outfield to shag fly balls. They would not let me in the batting cage, either. In fact, I was with the team about two weeks and I never got a chance to hit a baseball.

I traveled with the team to Cleveland, Detroit, and Chicago, and generally sat by Huggins during the ballgames. One incident in the Yankee dugout scared the hell out of me because I thought I was about to witness fisticuffs between teammates. Urban Shocker, a fine pitcher, passed down the dugout to get a drink of water. As he walked past Pat Collins, the tobacco-chewing catcher spit and painted an additional (brown) pinstripe from Shocker's shoulder all the way down his arm. I thought surely they would fight from the glares exchanged. Several innings later Shocker returned and as he came to where Collins sat, unloaded a mouthful of tobacco juice and water in Collins' face. Collins laughed and wiped his face. Everyone thought it was very funny—except me. Nothing at Duke had prepared me for this.

I am quite sure that Babe Ruth did not know that I existed, although we later became good friends when I joined the club for real in 1930. He was too busy playing ball and hitting the night spots, although not necessarily in that order.

The dugouts in Comiskey Park in Chicago had two rows of benches, and I sat behind Miller Huggins and Charley O'Leary, who were in the front row, so I could listen to what they had to say. One day Ruth did not show up for batting or fielding practice before the game. Huggins had already penciled him into the lineup and handed it to the umpires, and was fussing and fuming because the Babe had not shown up. Huggins said to O'Leary, "Charley, I'm going to fine him $5,000. I'm going to fine him if it's the last thing I do. I'm going to fine that big goon $5,000 for not showing up." Well, Babe showed up right before game time and played without any warmup. All he did that afternoon was hit two home runs and two doubles, driving in seven runs. After the ballgame I followed Huggins and O'Leary across the diamond to the other dugout to get to the visiting team clubhouse. Huggins just shook his head as he walked across the field, mumbling, "Charley, what in the hell am I going to do? What in the hell am I going to do? I can't fine him $5,000 now, the writers will eat me alive. What in the hell am I going to do?"

As odd as it might seem now to leave the team generally considered the greatest in baseball history to play in a summer league for a team in Newton, North Carolina, I did just that a week or so later. I went to Yankee general manager Ed Barrow and said, "Mr. Barrow, this arrangement is not working out to my benefit. I should be playing ball—hitting, running, fielding, and throwing in actual competition. I'm just like a wallflower, sitting on the bench listening to what Mr. Huggins says during ballgames. As far as I'm concerned it's a bad deal and I'm leaving. Thank you very much for the opportunity."

Mr. Barrow tried to talk me out of it, but I'd had enough. I left the ballclub and took the train to North Carolina. The New York papers made a big deal of my leaving the team. There were some articles written about the country kid from Berwyn turning his back on the league-leading Yankees. To me, though, it just made common sense. I had a job waiting for me to play everyday down in North Carolina and that is where I went. I was managed in Newton by Wade Lefler, who had played briefly for the pennant-winning 1924 Washington Senators. He was practicing law in Newton and was a Duke graduate, although he never mentioned the Duke connection to me.

I did not visit Yankee Stadium again until June, 1930. I was older then, twenty-two, with a bit more experience—three years at shortstop for the Duke varsity and three summers in good semipro leagues in Western Carolina, Virginia, and West Virginia. Upon receiving my diploma from Duke, I joined the Yankees at the Chase Hotel in St. Louis, just as agreed in 1927. I reported to manager Bob Shawkey, who had taken the position after the untimely death of Miller Huggins the previous September. Shawkey had pitched in the major leagues for fifteen years, the last twelve with the Yankees.

*Miller Huggins and Connie Mack—one died before his time
and the other lived to become the grand old man of baseball.*

He was polite, but didn't exactly welcome me with open arms. He gave me the impression that he was wondering what the hell was he going to do with this college kid. He assigned me a room with George "Yats" Wuestling, a utility infielder, and told me to report to Sportman's Park at 1:00 the following afternoon. I traveled by streetcar to the park, arriving at noon, a good hour before any other ballplayer. There was a locker with my name on it and in the locker a Yankee cap and gray road uniform. All the other necessities I had with me, including my prized black bat. I had hit .450 my senior year with it. I dressed, made my way to the visitor's dugout, and put my bat on the flat rack on the steps of the dugout.

About 1:30, the Yankees began to come noisily into the dugout and put their beautiful light-yellow ash Louisville Sluggers into the bat rack. My battered black bat was as out of place as a sunflower in the dead of winter. One of the Yankees soon noticed it and grabbed it by the handle, asking, "Who the hell's drugstore bat is this?" Without waiting for an answer, he tossed it forty or fifty feet out to the third base line. I could do nothing but dutifully retrieve my bat and keep my peace. The bat tosser turned out to be shortstop Lyn Lary, called "Broadway" by his teammates, probably because he was married to Broadway star Mary Lawler. Lary was a very good ballplayer and an all-right guy, but I did not learn this until later when I played beside him for the Boston Red Sox.

The 1930 Yankees were an outstanding ballclub, with Bill Dickey, Tony Lazzeri, Lary, Ben Chapman, Earle Combs, Red Ruffing, Harry Rice, and Gehrig and Ruth. But the players were much absorbed in catching the Philadelphia Athletics and Washington Senators, and they were largely indifferent to me. My roomie, Wuestling, was agreeable enough, but I mostly saw only his suitcase; he was never around in the evenings. The only ones to make me feel welcome were Dusty Cooke, Ben Chapman, and Herb Pennock. They asked me to join them for dinner and share taxicab rides to and from the ballparks. In Detroit, Pennock turned young Bob Carpenter over to me to take to the movies. Carpenter's father was president of DuPont and some years later bought the Philadelphia Phillies, installing son Bob as president and Pennock as general manager. Although Herb died suddenly in 1948, his handiwork resulted in the Whiz Kids' pennant of 1950.

Pennock was a Hall of Fame lefthanded pitcher and a fine gentleman. He gave me a bit of sound advice one day which I never forgot: "In this game, be nice to everyone on your way up, because you're going to meet a lot of them on your way down."

When I joined the Yankees, I truly believed I was going to move right in at shortstop. I had been blessed with considerable success playing college and semipro ball and I thought I was ready to take on the world. I was wrong. To do the job at the major league level, a player needs experience, and a lot of it. Although I was confident in my ability to play, I managed to freeze during my first at bat in the majors. It was a hot and muggy June day, and the second game of a doubleheader against the St. Louis Browns in Yankee Stadium before a boisterous capacity crowd. Lyn Lary had injured a thumb in the first game from a runner sliding into him at second base. Wuestling replaced Lyn but became ill from the heat and could not start the second game, so manager Shawkey informed me between games that I would play shortstop and bat second behind Earle Combs.

The opposing pitcher was George Blaeholder, the second most effective thrower on the Browns' staff. His first pitch was a fastball down the pipe that I took. Umpire Brick Owens bellowed STEE-RIIIKE so loud and so close to my ear that it scared the wits out of me. Blaeholder next threw a slider over the outside part of the plate. I wanted to swing, but my brain was not connecting with my hands and arms, so I took it for strike two. Brownie catcher Rick Ferrell had Blaeholder waste one outside at that juncture, thinking a rookie like me would go fishing and strike out on a bad pitch. I would have, too, but I could not move. I just stood there as another waste pitch sailed low and outside. Then, for some unexplicable reason, Blaeholder lost his control and threw two more balls. I stumbled down to first with a walk. If any of the last four pitches had crossed the plate, I would have struck out without lifting the bat off my shoulder. Babe Ruth was up next and he did what he did best, belting a home run, one of 49 that season, into the right-field bleachers, allowing me to score my first major league run in the process. My next time up my brain started functioning and I lined a single past Blaeholder's ear into center field. I followed that at-bat with another single and two more walks. I thus went two for two and reached base five times in my first big-league game. I also handled ten chances at shortstop without an error.

The next morning Ford Frick, the future Commissioner who was then a sportswriter, wrote that "Werber, in his first time at bat in big league competition, with two strikes on him watched the next four balls go by with the coolness of a veteran." Only my wife Tat knew the truth: I would have swung at all of them if I could have moved the bat.

The author shortly after joining the Yankees.

Skipper Miller Huggins—did he ever do battle with the Babe!

That first year I got into four games and hit .286 in 14 at-bats. I was not ready to play at the major league level, though, and Shawkey soon farmed me out to Albany of the Eastern League to gain experience under manager Bill McCorry. I hit about .350 and was selected the league's most valuable player. In 1931, I was promoted to the Toledo Mud Hens of the American Association, who were managed by Casey Stengel. I played poorly on a veteran club, did not get along well with Stengel, and was finally sent to the Newark Bears, the top Yankee farm club. There I was managed by Al Mamaux, who had been a 21-game winner for Pittsburgh in 1915 and 1916. I liked him even less than I did Stengel, and I did not play particularly well for the Bears.

In 1932, the Yankees sent me to play for the Buffalo Bisons under Ray Schalk, the old White Sox catcher. He was a fiesty little Dutchman and regaled us with stories of his eighteen years in the big leagues. He caught every game of the 1919 World Series for the so-called Black Sox against the Cincinnati Reds and was emphatic that Shoeless Joe Jackson and Ed Cicotte gave their best all the way. I always believed that as the catcher for the team, he was in a position to know.

Schalk was a fine manager and just let me play ball. I had a good year at bat and in the field, the team finished third in the tough International League, and I earned an invitation to Yankee spring training for 1933.

Upon arrival in St. Petersburg, Florida, I found I had plenty of competition awaiting me at shortstop. Frank Crosetti had been purchased by the Yankees from the San Francisco Seals and had mostly taken over the position from Lyn Lary in 1932. Lary, he of bat-throwing fame, had held the position for four years and though he had slipped a little in 1932 he still possessed a potent bat and good range in the field. Neither Crosetti nor Lary, however, could throw or hit as hard as I could, and I was the fastest afoot by good margin. Manager Joe McCarthy pretty much knew the abilities of Frank and Lyn, but he was not at all sure about me, so I played most of the exhibition games at shortstop. I thought I played pretty well, hitting .345 and running the bases aggressively. In the field, I caught everything hit my way, but some of my throws to first sailed past Gehrig and gave some concern to the patrons behind first base. Despite that, I thought I would be the Yankee shortstop.

After we broke camp at St. Petersburg, we played exhibition games in Birmingham and Memphis on the way north. Crosetti played shortstop, ostensibly so that a Red Sox scout named McAllister could evaluate him. Boston had finished dead last in 1932 with a horrendous record of 43-111. However, the team's new owner, Tom Yawkey, had a deep pocketbook and a love for baseball. He ordered his scouts to acquire young ballplayers who were not yet regulars from the top clubs and they were reportedly interested in Crosetti.

It gave McCarthy a chance to evaluate Crosetti as well, and after a few regular season games he decided to keep Frank and sell me to Boston, along with Dusty Cooke, Gordon Rhodes (another "Dusty," of course), Henry Johnson, and George Pipgras. Although I would have loved to stay with the Yankees, it is hard to fault McCarthy's decision. Crosetti went on to be the regular Yankees shortstop for the decade of the 1930s and played seventeen years for them overall.

It turned out all right for me as well. The Red Sox made me their regular third baseman, and after a seventh-place finish in 1933, we became quite respectable, finishing fourth the next three years. After a two-year stint with the Philadelphia Athletics, I was traded to Cincinnati just as the Reds were in a position to play for the pennant. Although I undoubtedly missed playing in a few World Series with the Yankees, I did get myself into two with the Reds.

2 THE BABE RUTH I REMEMBER

My first contact with Babe Ruth was during that short stretch I spent with the Yankees in 1927. He never knew I was there. When I returned to the team in 1930, though, I soon got to know him well and liked him very much. The Babe was a walking contradiction in terms. He was good natured, amoral, loving, loud, rough, vulgar, and kind and considerate of everyone, especially children.

When I walked in my first at-bat and was knocked in by Babe's homer, I decided to show off my speed. Art Fletcher, coaching third, was shouting, "Whoa, whoa" as I rounded third, but I kept running hard and probably scored before Ruth, with his peculiar little jog, reached first base. I sat down in the dugout and Ruth soon joined me. He said, "Son, you don't have to run when the Babe hits one."

The Babe had an unusual way of welcoming newcomers to the club, or at least he did in my case. Shortly after joining the Yankees, I was showering after the game, enjoying the lukewarm water and rinsing the soap from my face. All of a sudden I became aware of a warmer stream of water in the middle of my back. I turned to find Ruth using me as a temporary latrine, roaring with laughter.

I soon learned of the Babe's exceptional qualities. He absolutely adored children. His frequent visits to children's hospitals are now well known, but he conducted these visits privately, without the media. He did not want the press to take away from his time with the kids and he did not see the need to publicize his good deeds. Coming out of the Stadium after a ballgame, he would always stop and sign autographs for the kids who gathered there, sometimes for as long as an hour. He never turned a kid's autograph request down and he would sign until the last ragamuffin was satisfied. Although Babe drank plenty and smoked cigars, he never permitted his name to be used to endorse or promote alcohol or tobacco. He knew the kids looked up to him and he did not want to let them down.

Ruth was generous to a fault. He was always lending money to teammates and he made no effort to remember or total up who owed him what. One cold spring day at the Book-Cadillac Hotel in Detroit, Babe noticed that the Yankee clubhouse boy who had come up with us from Florida had no overcoat. Ruth peeled off a couple of $20 bills and told the lad to go buy himself a warm coat. In about half an hour the young man was back with his coat and he handed one of the bills back to Ruth. "Naw, keep it and buy yourself some good dinners," was the Babe's response. During spring training he would go to dinner with several of his teammates and always pick up the tab. During the season when he got ready to go to the ballpark, he would grab teammates who happened to be in the hotel lobby and say, "Let's go get a cab to the ballpark." Then he would insist on paying for the cab and the tip. He just would not take your money. Of course, Ruth was making about $80,000 a year, more than three times as much as other stars like Gehrig and Dickey. His teammates never resented the money the Babe made, however. We knew his high salary helped elevate our own wages. It also gave us the opportunity for some fun.

We were paid twice a month on the first and fifteenth. On payday, Mark Roth, the club secretary, would come through the clubhouse and lay a sealed envelope with the player's name typed on the front and his paycheck inside on the stool in front of each player's locker. Someone would invariably come along, slit Babe's envelope open and tape his check to the mirror over the sink for all the world to see. It came to about $7,500 a pay period, more than some players made all year. In fact, one afternoon Lyn Lary spied Ruth's paycheck on the mirror and yelled, "Hey Babe, I'll make

Clockwise from top: Jimmie Reese, Tony Lazzeri, Lyn Lary.

you a deal. I'll trade you my year's salary for this check." Babe just laughed and when he got ready to leave the clubhouse took the check down and stuck it into his wallet.

Although the Babe loved people, he was terrible at names and not much better at faces. He called almost everyone "keed" for kid. One story was that one day on the platform of the Back Bay Station as the team was preparing to leave Boston, teammate Tony Lazzeri introduced Myles Thomas to Babe as a new pitcher who had just joined the team from Harvard. Babe shook hands and welcomed him, "Glad to have you on the club, keed." At that juncture, Myles Thomas had been a relief pitcher on the team for several years.

Babe was very fond of Lazzeri, whom he affectionately called "Dago" or "Wop." To show their mutual affection, the two took turns destroying each other's gear, to their financial detriment. Fred Logan was the Yankee clubhouse man and he sold the players their inner hose, kangaroo-leather baseball shoes, and baseball undershirts, all at exorbitant prices. Ruth would take Doc Painter's scissors and cut the feet out of Lazzeri's inner hose. The next day Ruth would find his shoes nailed to the floor and the arms sliced out of his sweatshirt.

Like many ballplayers of the era, the Babe was very superstitious. On that 1930 Yankee team was a little reserve infielder named Jimmie Reese. Jimmie was always clowning around with Ruth. One day the Babe got irritated, pulled Reese's baseball shirt up around his shoulders, and hung him on a couple of hooks in the back of Reese's wire locker. There he stayed for a bit until Ruth took him down. Babe got several hits that day so the next day Reese was back hanging on his locker like a monkey, begging Ruth to put him down.

On another occasion, Ruth complained after batting practice to Yankee trainer Doc Painter that he was not seeing the ball very well. Doc suggested that Babe visit his medicine kit down by the water cooler and cleanse his eyes from a bottle of Eyelo solution. Ruth gave both eyes a shot and that afternoon went three for four. The next day the Babe put his name on the Eyelo bottle and loudly instructed one and all to stay away from his Eyelo. Babe continued his daily Eyelo bath and continued to hit. One day Lazzeri quietly poured all of the medicinal liquid out of the Eyelo bottle and filled it with water from the cooler. When Ruth began his eye bath ritual before the game, Lazzeri grabbed the bottle from his hand and drank its contents. Ruth guffawed, "Lookit the Dago, he's drinkin' the Baby's Eyelo." As it turned out, that day Tony got several hits. So thereafter, Babe washed *and* drank from the Eyelo bottle.

Although Babe might have been superstitious, he was, as everyone knows, an exceptional ballplayer, outstanding in all facets of the game. His wondrous power came from his very strong hands, wrists, and forearms. His approach to hitting was simple yet fascinating, as he related one day when he came into the dugout after crushing a ball far into the bleachers. Earle Combs asked him, "What kind of pitch did you hit, Babe?"

"Hell, I don't know what it was," Babe responded, "It sure went out of here, didn't it?"

Then he went on to expound on his theory of hitting: "The trouble with you guys is that you are always worried about what pitch you're going to get; a fastball, a curve, a changeup, or a sinker. When I go up there to hit, I don't think about nuthin'. I just hit what they throw up there."

Off the field, Ruth liked to play bridge and was good at it. He learned that I played, and Lou Gehrig and he would pair off against Bill Dickey and me on our train rides between cities. Although this was during Prohibition, Babe always had a fifth of Seagram's along. (Whiskey was presumably available to any ballplayer who wanted it, but I can recall no one except Babe who ever had any.) He would sip it from a glass with ice and a little water and would imbibe six to eight ounces in a couple of hours. He could hold his liquor and was never inebriated but the routine was inevitably the same. Once he had made serious inroads into the Seagram's and began to feel jocular, Babe would begin to make ridiculous, or as he called them, "phoncky" bids, just to irritate Gehrig. Lou was an excellent bridge player, better than Ruth, and took the game seriously. When Ruth started getting phoncky, Lou would throw in his cards, saying, "The game's over, add up the score."

Ruth would give Gehrig the big raspberry, "Pfffffft." Babe could really give the raspberry; it sounded like a busted balloon. Then he would say, "Up your gingee, up your gingee." Dickey always kept score, so he would total the points. Though we played for small stakes, Dickey and I always won three or four dollars. Then the next train ride, Babe would say, "Let's play some bridge," and we would repeat the scenario.

Babe was a first-rate practical joker and would go to great lengths to pull one off. On one occasion, Ruth picked Ed Wells, a tall, angular left-handed pitcher, for one of his creative badger games. Ed had come to the Yankees in 1929 from the Detroit organization and was quiet, but a man

Bill Dickey, the brains of the ballclub.

Ed Wells—a unwilling victim of the badger caper.

of exemplary habits. He was single but was planning to marry a girl from Alabama at the end of the season. We had played a day game in Detroit when Babe began imploring Ed to double date with him that evening. Ed was at first unwilling, saying he was tired from pitching that afternoon. It was only his reluctance to displease the Babe and Babe's assurance that the girls were all right that finally led him to go along. Ruth told him the girls liked to drink and to bring a fifth of gin; Ruth would buy a bag of oranges for a mix. So armed, the players set out in a taxi for a house in the suburbs. As they arrived and walked up to the house, Babe held the gin and Ed the bag of oranges. The house was dark but Ruth opened the screen door to the porch and rang the door bell. The door opened, but instead of an attractive female to greet them, they came face to face with a big ugly male, half again the size of the Babe. "So you're the scum who've been after my wife," he bellowed. "I oughta kill ya." With that he pulled out a snub-nosed pistol and fired point blank at Ruth.

"I'm hit, Ed," Babe screamed as he collapsed on the porch, "Run. Run for your life, Ed. Run."

Wells bolted straight through the screen door with oranges flying in all directions. Expecting to be hit in the back with a bullet at any moment, he turned the wrong way and under a full head of steam ran into a board fence protecting some excavation work. Picking himself up, he tore back past the house from whence he had come, with no sign of the mortally wounded Ruth.

Several hours later, shaken and disheveled, Ed made it back to the Book Cadillac Hotel where the Yankees stayed. Although the lobby had been singularly free of Yankee ballplayers when Ed and Babe had left earlier in the evening, it was full of them now, all with grim faces. Lazzeri spoke first, "Ed, Babe's been shot. He's in bad shape and asking for you." Then several teammates took Ed up to Ruth's dimly lit room, where the home run king was laid out on his bed, talcum powder on his face and ketchup generously applied to his white shirt.

"He's dying," said Earle Combs mournfully. The scene was too much for the Ed, who passed out on the spot. It took some time before the uproarious players and guffaws of the very much alive Babe could convince the panic-stricken Wells that he had not witnessed the murder of the most famous person in America. Even later we never could persuade Ed of the humor in the situation.

The Babe was, of course, a legend with the ladies. One chilly, drizzly spring training morning in St. Petersburg in 1933, several of us were sitting around a potbellied stove in the clubhouse, waiting to hear whether manager Joe McCarthy was going to call off practice or not. Earle Combs, Tony Lazzeri, Bill Dickey, and I were in various stages of dress and Ruth had on only a sweatshirt. Lazzeri, who was a great agitator, asked Ruth, "Tell us about that Latin broad from Ybor City who shot you, Babe."

Ruth edged his big flat feet closer to the stove, spit some tobacco juice and said, "Ah, that wasn't much." He then proceeded to tell us the story. Babe liked to come down to spring training early to play golf and, it turns out, chase women. Several years before he had been seeing a girl from Ybor City when something better came along. He told the first young woman that he had to go into training and would not be able to see her any more in the evenings. With her Latin temper she "got burnt up and raised a scene," but Babe said he got her quieted down and thought that was the end of it. One evening shortly thereafter he was having dinner with the new flame at the Temple Terrace Country Club, near Tampa. They were sitting by French doors looking over the golf course. All of a sudden the Latin girl came in the door and spied Babe having dinner with her replacement. With fire in her eyes she walked toward Babe and, as she walked, she took a revolver out of her purse.

"Then what happened?" asked Tony.

"Hell," said Babe, "I took those French doors right with me, glass, wood, curtains and all."

"What did she do?"

"She shot me! I didn't feel anything for a mile or two but she shot me. Look at this." Babe turned his leg and showed us a large scar just below his left calf. "Ain't that a beauty."

"Did you prosecute her," Dickey wanted to know.

"Naw, she was a nice gal," was Babe's response.

The Babe's good humor was legendary. You could, however, push him too far. In fact, the Babe's famous called shot in the 1932 World Series probably never would have happened if Mark Koenig had not crossed the line with Babe when the two were teammates with the Yankees. Koenig was a rough, tough ballplayer who became the regular shortstop for the Yankees in 1926. One day in the clubhouse early in 1929, before I was with the club, Ruth apparently announced that he was going to marry Claire Hodgson, whom he had been seeing for several years. Koenig piped up and said, "Babe, you don't want to marry her. Half the guys in the American League have slept with her." That was not true, of course, and Babe defended Claire's honor, hauling off and belting Koenig. Koenig would fight anybody, so he went after Ruth and their teammates had to separate them.

By early the following year, Koenig had been traded to the Detroit Tigers. The speculation was that the altercation with Ruth had something to do with the Yankees unloading him. He ended up back with his hometown San Francisco Missions in the Pacific Coast League in 1932. In August, he was purchased by the Chicago Cubs to play shortstop after Billy Jurges was shot in his hotel room by an estranged girlfriend. Koenig went on to hit .353 and was a key figure in the Cubs' drive to the National League pennant.

When the Cubs met to vote their World Series shares just before the Series, they voted Koenig only a half share. (Rogers Hornsby, who had managed the club for two-thirds of the year before being fired, got nothing.) Koenig had been a popular Yankee and this slighting enraged his former teammates, who verbally let loose at the "cheapskate" Cubs from the

Series opener. The Cubs responded in kind, with most of their assault aimed at the Babe.

All of that jawing back and forth reached a crescendo in the fifth inning of Game 3 in Wrigley Field when Ruth allegedly called his shot against Charlie Root and hit a mammoth line-drive home run into the center-field bleachers on a two-two pitch. I cannot say whether the Babe actually called his shot, since I was not with the ballclub at the time. But the entire incident might not have occurred if Koenig had kept his trap shut in the Yankee clubhouse three years before.

With that one understandable exception, Babe's good nature seemingly never wavered, at least while I was around. For example, on one occasion Babe was observing a bridge game on the train and getting immense pleasure out of needling Dusty Cooke, one of the participants. Finally Dusty, who was a big, strapping outfielder, got fed up and proceeded to grab Ruth, lift him, and shove him into an upper berth in the Pullman. No one got a bigger kick out of the manhandling than Babe himself.

Perhaps that explains my reaction when Ruth used me as a temporary urinal that day in the shower. No, I did not hit Babe or even yell at him. I just laughed along with him. It was almost a badge of honor in a perverse sort of way. It meant that he had accepted me as a Yankee.

3 TO TAKE FATE, OR WHATEVER THE GODS MAY GIVE

Dusty Cooke. You will not find his name in the Baseball Hall of Fame and present-day sportswriters have probably never heard of him, but he was denied baseball immortality by a quirk of fate. Christened Allen Lindsay Cooke, he was a big guy, six-foot-two and 205 pounds. He was all bone and muscle, hard as a rock and strong as an ox. I know. I liked to wrestle with him and he was always careful not to do me harm. It was fortunate that he was a good-natured fellow as well, which is why Babe Ruth liked to pester him. He handled Ruth like a 50-pound sack of corn in the Pullman car that day.

When I quizzed Dusty about his display of strength in stuffing Babe into the upper berth, he dismissed it as of little consequence, noting that he was the runt of the litter. He went on to describe his brother Vincent who stood in at six-foot-five and weighed 250 pounds. Seems that Vincent was out on the farm plowing a field behind a mule. The mule would work awhile and stand awhile. No amount of harassment could move the mule until he decided to move. Completely losing his patience at last, Vincent moved to the front of the mule, grabbed it by the ears with both hands and bit it on the nose until blood came. According to Dusty, that was the last bit of trouble that mule ever gave Vincent. Those North Carolina boys were tough.

Dusty was signed by the Yankees out of the North Carolina sandlots and sent to the Asheville Tourists of the Sally League in 1928. With his future Yankee teammate Ben Chapman at shortstop and Dusty roaming the outfield, Asheville finished with a 97-49 won-lost record and won the pennant by a mere 18 games. Promoted with Chapman to St. Paul of the American Association the following year, Cooke won the league's Triple Crown, with a .358 batting average, 33 home runs, and 148 runs batted in.

In 1930, at the tender age of 23, Dusty made the Yankees. He appeared in 92 games, hitting a modest .255. He hit his stride the following spring and was battling his old minor-league teammate Chapman for a starting position in the Yankee outfield alongside Combs and Ruth. He was hitting .333 when, on April 28 at Griffith Stadium in Washington, disaster struck. Playing right field against the Senators, Dusty separated his shoulder trying to make a diving catch of a drive off the bat of Ossie Bluege. He was through for the year. The separation was a severe one and Cooke went to Johns Hopkins University Hospital for repair. Dr. George Bennett, the leading orthopedic surgeon of the day, had to reconstruct Dusty's arm and shoulder joint by taking fascia from his thigh, drilling holes in his arm and shoulder bones, and connecting them with the borrowed tissue. The 1931 season was a loss, as was 1932 when he appeared in only three games. In the spring of 1933, the Yankees sold Dusty, George Pipgras, and me to the Boston Red Sox. Coming back from his severe injury, Cooke simply could not run as fast, throw as well, or hit with as much authority or power as before his injury. He was never the same ballplayer.

It was my good fortune to room with Dusty for the next four years on all the Red Sox road trips, as well as at the Sheraton Hotel in Boston when my family was not in town. No finer gentleman ever lived. In the years we roomed together, he never once complained of his ill fortune. Once in a while, however, Dusty would become depressed about the effects of his injury and would quietly nurse a bottle of Jack Daniels. On these infrequent resorts to alcohol, he would invariably fall out of bed. I could not lift him to get him back into bed, so I would just cover him with blankets and let him sleep on the floor. The next morning Dusty would be his usual pleasant self with nothing said of the evening of alcohol-induced sleep.

Dusty Cooke and the author with the Red Sox.
He was as good a friend as I had in baseball.

In the off-season Dusty was an avid quail hunter. He loved to go afield in his native North Carolina with bird dogs and a shotgun to hunt for this elusive bird. Many bird hunters dislike cats, wild or tame, because they deplete the wild bird population, and Dusty was no exception. He had a phobia about cats which was well known to all his Red Sox teammates.

Near the end of the 1933 season, the Red Sox were purchased by Thomas Austin Yawkey, a Detroit millionaire. One of Mr. Yawkey's projects to revitalize the franchise was to renovate Fenway Park. New seats were installed, both visitor and home locker rooms and showers were improved, the playing field was put into top condition, and, since Yawkey owned a paint company, the entire park got a fresh coat. We were to play an exhibition game against the Boston Braves immediately before the start of the 1934 season, but a cold drizzle forced cancellation. Several of us were anxious to see the renovations, so we put on our overcoats and walked over to the ballpark from the Sheraton Hotel on Back Bay Road. While some of the men stopped to look over the visiting team clubhouse, Roy Johnson, Rick Ferrell, Bob Seeds, and I moved on to the Red Sox locker room. There Ferrell flipped on the light switch in the shower room and discovered several wild cats, probably attracted by rats, pigeons, and food scraps from the workmen.

Rick could barely wait to fetch Dusty to the scene. Armed with a broom that someone found, and with malice aforethought, Dusty immediately went to work trying to eliminate the cats. The rest of us stood on stools taken from inside the lockers to view the show since we did not want those wild cats charging us or, worse, trying to climb up one of our legs. The newly installed floors and locker tops were still covered with construction dust, making traction for the cats difficult until propelled along by one of Cookie's swipes with the broom. Soon they were on tops of the lockers with Cooke swinging at them like a man fighting a swarm of bees, except this encounter was to the whoops and laughter of his teammates. The room became so choked with dust that Dusty, coat unbuttoned and hat askew, took on the look of Lawrence of Arabia riding a camel in a sandstorm. The cats finally escaped through a window in the rear of the clubhouse with about enough clearance for a mouse. Dusty was sweating profusely and was, if nothing else, convinced that tomcats are tough to kill with a broom.

Dusty played with the Red Sox through the 1936 season before spending 1937 with the Minneapolis Millers in the American Association. He hit a resounding .345 in 151 games, earning a trip back to the big leagues in 1938, this time with Cincinnati. Although he batted a respectable .275 in 82 games with the improving Reds, 1938 was to be his swansong as a major league player. He was thirty-one years old.

Cooke hit a robust .340 with the Rochester Red Wings of the International League in 1939, but even that performance could not earn him a trip back to the majors. He played out the string with the Jersey City Giants and Rochester through 1942 before serving in World War II.

When Cooke returned from the war, his old friend Ben Chapman was managing the Philadelphia Phillies under general manager Herb Pennock, another teammate from his Yankee and Red Sox days. Chapman hired him as the Phillies' trainer in 1946, apparently expanding on some of Dusty's military experience. He became a coach for Chapman in 1948, and when Ben was fired midway through the season, Dusty became interim manager and piloted the club until Eddie Sawyer was named skipper.

Sawyer had been managing the Phillies' top farm team at Toronto, but had no major league experience as a player or manager. In an unusual move, but one that made sense given his lack of experience, he kept all of Chapman's coaches, including Cooke. Dusty remained with the Phillies until Sawyer was fired in 1952. He was the first-base coach for the pennant-winning 1950 Whiz Kids.

After baseball, Dusty and his wife Daphne operated a novelty shop full of glassware and bric-a-brac back in North Carolina. He died November 21, 1987, at the age of eighty after a series of strokes. Not all the good ones are in the Baseball Hall of Fame.

4 OF HAIR LOSS, FISH GUTS AND THE BROTHERS FERRELL

Brothers Richard (Rick) Benjamin Ferrell and Wesley Cheek Ferrell were two of the finest ballplayers of the 1930s and two of my best friends in baseball. They must have been good friends because I managed a pretty sweet prank on each of them, as I will relate. Between the two they spent thirty-three years in the big leagues. Rick and Wes were two of seven brothers from a farm near Guilford, North Carolina. Another one of their brothers, George, had a twenty-year minor league career.

Rick did the catching for the Boston Red Sox from 1933 though 1936. I played third base for the Red Sox during those years, and he and I hung out together. Overall he caught in the big leagues for eighteen years and never played an inning at any other position. Rick was one of the finest receivers of his day and was durable, setting an American League record with 1,805 games behind the plate. At bat, he had a fine eye, walking 937 times in his career while striking out only 277 times and achieving an impressive .433 on-base percentage. Selected to the American League All-Star team seven times, Rick could hit a little, too, compiling a rock solid .281 career batting average. He earned his way into the Hall of Fame.

Rick was quite a competitor on the field, but off of it he was generally the soul of equanimity. During our time as teammates, he was a handsome, young, unmarried fellow who was gradually growing bald with a receding hairline. We played a lot of bridge on train trips in those days, with Rick teaming up with brother Wes and me with Dusty Cooke. Wesley was an aggressive bidder, so Rick was the dummy more than his share of the time. While he quietly watched Wes get set, he would massage the sides of his scalp with his fingers. We'd give him a hard time, telling him time after time, "You can't get hair to grow in concrete." Rick would respond defensively, "It brings circulation into my scalp which will make my hair grow." This went on all summer. During the winter I got my hair cut at Bill Peterson's barber shop on 14th St., N.W., a bit above G Street in Washington. Bill was from Shelby, North Carolina, and a ball fan. While being made pretty one day, I told him about Ferrell's attempt to grow hair by massaging his head. "No way," he said, and while walking back to the office I decided to have some fun come next season at the expense of Rick's head. I obtained some of Bill Peterson's barber shop stationary, enlisted his involvement, and had typed on it this fairy tale:

> I read about your problem of diminishing hair on the sport page of the Washington *Post* and can appreciate your concern. If you will contact me next season on one of your club's several trips to D.C., I'll be happy to discuss with you the remedial treatment I have available. For the reasonable sum of $300, I can guarantee hair restoration.
>
> "I am a graduate of the University of North Carolina's School of Pharmacology, Class of 1930, and will be most happy to be of service to you.
>
> Sincerely,
> William G. Peterson

On the first day of spring training in 1935, Rick sought me out about a William G. Peterson in Washington, D.C., who guaranteed to grow hair for $300. "Sure," I said, "I know the guy and if he told you that he can induce growth, then he can do it." Rick got a check off to Peterson posthaste, but here my carefully orchestrated plan went astray. Peterson returned the check to Rick. The District of Columbia had stopped hair restoration treatments, he said, so he was temporarily not in a position to keep his commitment. He also wrote to me advising me that if the scam went through he thought he might end up in jail. The things friends do to each other! The horror of it is that I cannot remember after all these years whether we intended to keep the money or return it.

Rick's brother Wesley Ferrell should be in the Hall of Fame but, for reasons that escape me, it does not look like he will ever make it. All he did was pitch in the big leagues for fifteen years with a record of 193-128 for a winning percentage of .601.He won 190 of those victories in a remarkable streak of ten years, from 1929 through 1938.

Wes also was probably the best-hitting pitcher of all time, ending his career with a .280 batting average and an impressive .446 slugging average. His career 38 home runs is still the record for pitchers. In 1935, he hit a cool .347 in 150 at bats and clubbed seven homers. He was such a good hitter that he was used as a pinch hitter 139 times during his career.

Wesley was born on February 2, 1908, two years and about four months after his brother Rick. My association with Wes began in my first year at Duke University when our freshman baseball team, the Blue Imps, had a game against the Oak Ridge Academy. We were well aware of the prowess of the Oak Ridge pitcher, a tough egg named Ferrell, before the team ever arrived to play us. Although Ferrell was said to be headed to the big leagues, the Blue Imps were not too shabby a freshman team: seven of us would eventually sign to play professional baseball. We managed to beat Wes that day before an overflow crowd at Haynes Field.

Shortly thereafter, Wesley left Oak Ridge to sign with the Cleveland Indians. He was barely nineteen, stood a well-proportioned six-foot-two, and possessed a mean fastball and an outstanding curve. The Indians farmed him out for the summers of 1927 and 1928, but brought him to the majors to pitch in 1929 at the age of twenty-one. All he did was win 21 games, second most in the league, while losing just ten for the third-place

Wes Ferrell—Hollywood good looks and a temper to match.

Indians. He followed that impressive debut with seasons of 25, 22, and 23 wins.Not even the great Lefty Grove won 91 games his first four years in the majors.

In 1933, Ferrell hurt his arm and won but 11 games for the Indians, who thought he was through. Tom Yawkey had obtained Rick Ferrell from the St. Louis Browns soon after he purchased the Boston Red Sox. After catching the Boston pitching staff in 1933, Rick hightailed it to the front office and persuaded general manager Eddie Collins to part with some of Mr. Yawkey's money and obtain old, washed-up Wesley.

It was when Wes reported for spring training in 1934 that I finally got to know him, although I had followed his career from that day he had pitched for Oak Ridge against the Blue Imps. I quickly learned that he was a competitor from the word go and, although he no longer had his former fastball, he was hardly through. He won 14 and lost 5 for the Red Sox in 1934, and followed that with a 25-win season in 1935 and a 20-win season in 1936.

Ferrell wanted the ball, and if he was not pitching, he wanted to pinch hit. In the late innings of a close ball game, Wesley could sense when a pinch hitter might be needed almost before the manager. He would go to the bat rack, select his bat, and walk to and fro in front of manager Bucky Harris, waving that bat. He wanted to be at the plate no matter who was pitching and he could be counted on to get the bat on the ball. He even played 13 games in the outfield in 1934 and hit .282 for the year.

Sometimes Wesley was too much the competitor. One afternoon in Shibe Park, he had the A's down, 10-0, in their half of the sixth inning. They touched him for five runs, but Harris seemed unworried. Ferrell was a smart pitcher and he was always a threat with the bat. In the seventh, however, the A's scored four more and Harris finally walked to the mound to get the ball. Wesley just turned his back and walked out toward short-stop. When Harris finally managed to corral him and get him into the dugout, Ferrell struck himself in the jaw with his fist and slammed his head into the concrete wall. Bucky had to pin his arms to his sides to keep him from doing further damage. Another time I saw him get so mad after being taken out of a game that he jumped up and down on an expensive watch he owned, crunching it beyond repair.

Wesley did not like to lose at anything. Since Dusty and I were better bridge players, the two Ferrell brothers inevitably paid us three or four dollars on every train ride. It was only tip money to the Ferrells, whose salaries were larger than Dusty's and mine. Inevitably after a few bad hands, Wesley would smash the end of the deck of cards against the Pullman table, yell for the porter, and pay for a new deck. He could not stand losing even at bridge.

Wes was a strikingly handsome fellow, with blue eyes, blond wavy hair, and an engaging personality—when he was not mad about something. By this time he had already been to Hollywood for screen tests, but did not like the Hollywood personalties he encountered and quickly returned to resume his baseball career.

He was single and, not surprisingly, attractive to the ladies. In Sarasota for spring training in 1935, he rented a nice-looking Chevrolet to use for fishing and, he hoped, for dates. There it sat in front of the Sarasota Terrace Hotel on one very warm spring day, awaiting Wesley and his dinner date that evening. One of the wags on the Red Sox decided to have a little fun and retrieved from the hotel's garbage a double handful of fish guts and crab leavings. He wrapped the whole mess in a folded newspaper and stuffed it behind the rear seat of Wesley's car, where it festered all day under the warm Florida sun. The car was not only not habitable for the evening, it may have never been habitable again. Our manager in 1935 was Joe Cronin, who had a clubhouse meeting every day before our morning workout. This one Ferrell took over. Pulling his stool from his locker, he stood on it to be better seen and heard, and with flushed face and contorted mouth announced that if the no-good louse who had stunk up his car was man enough to admit it, he would whip him right then and there. With spit flying and eyes ablaze, he said if two had done it, he would lick them both.

"Tell 'em," his teammates shouted. "Whup 'em. Get 'em all." No one, however, stepped forward to admit responsibility. Old Wesley was not much known as a fighter, but that day he might have been a formidable opponent. And, of course, no one thought a clubhouse fight would do anybody any good, so we just let Wes rant and rave a while.

Whether it was the car incident, minor but constant losses at bridge, or too much fishing on Lake Myaka, I am not certain, but Wesley's spring-training outings that year were abominable. He just could not get anyone out. After each miserable showing he would assure Joe Cronin, "Don't worry, Joe. I'll be ready for Opening Day. I want that opening game." Our opener was against the New York Yankees in Yankee Stadium. There would be a crowd of about 65,000 in the ballpark, just the kind of setting that Wesley loved. Joe would then ask me in confidence, "How the hell can I start that guy Opening Day? He can't get anybody out." In spite of it all, Wesley ultimately talked Joe into starting him. It was a chilly April day in New York with swirling winds. The pitching mound in Yankee Stadium was too high, Wesley could not get comfortable on it, and he walked the first two men. He asked for time, laid down his glove, and attacked the mound with spikes flying. He was soon almost lost in a cloud of whirling dust and dirt. Art Fletcher, the Yankee third-base coach, was hollering, "Tear it up, Wesley. Want me to get you a shovel?" The mound finally to his liking, Wesley picked up his glove, took a couple of warm up pitches, and beat Lefty Gomez, 1-0. He ended up winning 25 games for Joe Cronin in 1935, not bad for a pitcher Cleveland turned loose for peanuts.

They did not all go like that. Wesley always wanted to pitch in Cleveland, against the club that had turned him loose for one bad year after he had won 20 or more games his first four seasons there. He especially liked to pitch on Sundays before the big crowds. One such Sunday turned into disaster. Wes got off to a bad start when umpire Lou Kolls was seemingly unable to distinguish between balls and strikes, and so just called everything a ball. Wes blew his top and Kolls tossed him from the game after a jowl-to-jowl encounter with spit a-flying. Brother Rick Ferrell was catching, and was as noted for his equanimity of disposition as his younger brother was for his tempestuousness. But the bad calls and his brother's ejection were too much. He popped his cork and got in Kolls' face as well. Kolls gave him the heave-ho, too, at which time Rick threw his mask into the netting behind home plate, threw his glove out somewhere beyond the pitching mound, and a shin guard toward each dugout. All the while the occupants of both dugouts were cheering each display of temper. When Wesley came into our dugout, he took a pair of scissors from Doc Logan's training bag, sat, and began to cut his glove into a thousand pieces.

Each time he cut a piece, he would utter a grunt. We watched in bemused silence, not wanting to disturb him with those scissors in his hand.

I loved old Wesley. He was a good man. He and Rick went back to their mother and dad's dairy farm after every season and used their baseball earnings to equip it with the most modern machinery. He could also pitch and was a tough competitor. He wanted to win, hated losing, and tried hard all the time.

Wes Ferrell died in Sarasota, Florida, in 1976 at the all too tender age of 68. And he never did find out who put the fish guts behind the rear seat of his Chevrolet back in 1935. I guess it is too late to tell him that I did it.

5 FIGHTS AND NEAR-FIGHTS

Baseball in the 1930s was, as now, a highly competitive game with young men giving their all for victory. The pressure, particularly in the heat of a pennant race played before large crowds, was immense. The games were mostly played in the dog days of summer and so it is not surprising that tempers were often lost in the middle of contests with fisticuffs the result. Even among teammates familiarity sometimes bred contempt. A team spent a lot of time together during the six months of the season with train travel, lobby sitting, and time at the ballpark. Twenty-five competitive young men could not really be expected to get along all the time and, in my day, they did not.

It is important to remember that professional baseball players are not fighters. Rarely in the over a hundred years of baseball competition have two antagonists stood toe to toe and slugged it out with clenched fists. Mostly, baseball fights consist of players grabbing each other's shirts to keep from getting hit. Very little blood has dripped onto the grass of a ball diamond from fisticuffs.

Sometimes, in the heat of battle, the most unlikely ballplayer could go over the edge. For example, Bill Dickey, the Yankees' great catcher, was friendly, affable, and easy to get along with. When the baseball season was over he returned to his beloved Arkansas, oiled his shotguns, worked his bird dogs, and took to the fields after the elusive bob-white quail. Later, when retired from baseball he was successful in the investment field in Little Rock.

Carl Reynolds was a big, raw-boned Texan from the metropolitis of LaRue. Although forgotten today, Carl was a fine big-league outfielder, compiling a .302 batting average in thirteen seasons with the White Sox, Senators, Browns, Red Sox, and Cubs. In 1930, he hit .359 with 22 home runs and 100 runs batted in. He could run with anyone in the league and stole 112 bases in his career, a high total for the 1930s. He was a real gentleman, well liked, and although quiet, he smiled easily.

So how is it possible for two classy men like Dickey and Reynolds to get into a fight, which unfortunately caused one so much pain and the other so much remorse? I guess the Dickey-Reynolds fight just goes to show that it can happen to anyone. It really was not so much of a fight as Dickey's fist smashing into Reynold's jaw and breaking it. It happened on the Fourth of July, 1932 when Reynolds' Senators were playing Dickey's Yankees at Griffith Stadium. Not long before, Roy Johnson of the Red Sox had jarred Dickey with a body block in a play at home plate, injuring his kidneys and sidelining him for a good stretch. A few days after his return, a throw to the plate was high and Bill had to jump and extend to reach it. Eric McNair of the Athletics was the runner and instead of sliding, gave Dickey a cross-body block to his midsection, knocking him flying. After that Dickey decided enough was enough and determined to lay out the next player coming in to rough him up. That player happened to be Carl Reynolds. He knocked Dickey down in a collision at the plate, causing him to drop the ball. Carl picked himself up and headed for the dugout. Dickey regained his feet, rushed at Reynolds from behind and in a cold fury threw a hard right, connecting with full force against Carl's jaw. The injury knocked Reynolds, who was hitting .360, out of the lineup for six weeks. Judge Landis reacted swiftly, suspending Dickey for thirty days and fining him the very hefty sum of $1,000. Bill, if anything, punished himself even more. He felt so badly about hitting Carl that he apologized to him personally and in the press, and insisted on paying all of Carl's medical expenses.

It could have been worse. Soon afterward, while riding in a taxicab with his wife one afternoon, Carl started to choke. With a rare degree of coolness, she reached into her purse, took out a small pair of scissors and cut the wires holding his jaws together.

A real brawl between the Yankees and Senators exploded on April 25, 1933, when Ben Chapman of the Yankees slid with spikes high into Buddy Myer at second base to break up a double play. There were still bad feelings between the teams from the Dickey-Reynolds incident the year before. A few days earlier, Myer had slid into Lou Gehrig knee-high at first base, ripping Lou's uniform and spiking him. Even Babe Ruth got caught up in the hostilities, crashing into Joe Cronin on a play at third and nearly coming to blows when Joe expressed his objection.

After Chapman's aggressive slide, Myer got up and kicked Ben in the back. Chapman was a big strong, muscular fellow, mean as a snake, and he tore into Myer. Both benches emptied and fights broke out all over the field. Dixie Walker in particular rushed from the Yankee bench and attacked Myer with a running jump from behind. Washington fans piled out of the stands, swinging at anything in a Yankee uniform. The police had to come down from the stands and it took about twenty minutes to get things settled down.

Lefty Gomez was a tall, slight fellow, not at all strong and robust. A Senator got him from behind, and Don Brennan, a big burly pitcher for the Yankees, yanked the guy off. Gomez turned around and swung at the Washington player but coldcocked Brennan instead, knocking him for a gallyloop.

Chapman, Myer, and Walker were kicked out of the game. To leave the field, Chapman and Walker had to go right by the Washington dugout to enter a tunnel to the Yankee clubhouse. When they did, Earl Whitehill, a pitcher for the Senators with his own reputation for aggressiveness, yelled at Chapman, "You're a no good southern sonuvabitch." So Chapman went after Whitehill and clipped him with a right to the left side of his face. The fact that Chapman was in the middle of the Washington dugout did not faze him. Chapman and Walker battled about a dozen Senators down the steps to the Yankee dressing room. For the second time, benches emptied and fights broke out all over. The police again had to restore order.

Restoring Washington's pride was another matter as they lost the ball-game, 16-0, to Yankee rookie pitcher Russ Van Atta. Van Atta truly had a debut to dream about, also going 4 for 4 at the plate. His shutout that day would be the only one he would throw in a seven-year big-league career.

During both rhubarbs Babe Ruth remained on the Yankee bench, watching with an amused expression on his face and in total quietude. After the fighting subsided, some of the players asked him, "Babe, why didn't you get off of the bench and get in this thing?" The Babe said, "Jake don't pay me to fight. Jake pays me to hit home runs." Of course, he meant Jacob Ruppert, the Yankee owner.

For their trouble, American League President Will Harridge suspend-ed Chapman, Myer, and Whitehill for five days and fined them $100 apiece. My old friend Dixie Walker managed to emerge from the fracas without sanction.

I must report that the Senators did indeed have the last laugh in 1933. They took the league lead from New York on June 23 and, led by Cronin, Myer, Heinie Manush, Goose Goslin, and Earl Whitehill's 22 wins (General Crowder had 24 to lead the staff), swept to the pennant, seven games in front of the Yankees.

Buddy Myer was a fine ballplayer and a good friend of mine who bat-ted over .300 nine times in a seventeen-year big league career. He liked a bat I'd given him so much that he ordered duplicates. He won the 1935 Amercan League batting title on the last day of the season, going 3 for 4 to finish at .3495. He nosed out Cleveland's Joe Vosmik, who sat out the first game of a doubleheader the last day of the season to protect his lead. When word got to Cleveland about Myer's hot hitting, Vosmik played the second game. He could muster only 1 for 4 and finished at .3489, six thousandths of a point behind Buddy, who was using my model bat.

Myer was one of the finest bunters ever to play, and as a left-handed hitter he was particularly adept at dragging the ball for a base hit. He is said to have beaten out 60 bunts one season.

Although Myer was a good friend of mine, that did not stop us from getting into a brawl with each other. It happened in 1936, when I was playing for Connie Mack in Philadelphia. Mr. Mack had a history of giving young, untested players a quick big-league baptism, particularly college boys. On this occasion the Athletics were playing Washington and Mr. Mack inserted Hal Wagner, a young catcher out of Duke University, behind the plate. Wagner would become a solid big league catcher, but at this point in his career his attitude needed some adjustment. When Myer, the reigning American League batting champion, mildly protested a called strike, Wagner responded from behind the plate, "Aw, shut up. That ball was down the gut." A rookie catcher just does not run his mouth to an established star. Myer quickly stepped out of the batter's box and told Wagner what he thought of him in no uncertain terms. On the following pitch, Buddy singled. The next batter smashed a long double and Myer raced into home plate intent on doing bodily harm to young Wagner. He hit Hal in the chest with both spikes, knocking him cold and cutting him in the throat and collarbone. Both benches emptied but aside from some pushing and shoving, no punches were thrown. Wagner had to be carried into the clubhouse to be patched up.

During Myer's next at-bat, Bud Thomas, our pitcher, low-bridged him with a fastball, sending Buddy's cap flying. Tempers were high on both sides and Myer was burning. He again singled, was sacrificed to second, and soon took off toward me in an attempted steal of third. The throw by Charley Berry, who had taken over for Wagner behind the plate, was right on the bag. As I heard the umpire bawl, "You're out," I jumped away from the bag to throw the ball to Skeeter Newsome at shortstop. It was then I noticed blood trickling down my forearm, a result of Myer's spikes. I certainly did not regard it as an accident and so whirled and connected with a solid right to Buddy's cheekbone. Although I was unaware of it at the time, from then on I was substantially hampered by Clyde Milan, the Senator's third-base coach, who had leaped on my back as I tried to jump on Myer.

Fights broke out all over the infield. Berry, well insulated by his face mask, chest protector, and shin guards, swung at Goose Goslin, breaking his nose. Joe Krakauskas, a 200-pounder, charged from the Washington dugout and was promptly belted and knocked flat by our left fielder Bob Johnson. Krakauskas' cap floated down after he did, coming to rest on his chest. Meanwhile, Myers was running the bases in reverse, throwing punches at everyone he encountered and getting clobbered again near second base by little Dario Lodigiani, our second baseman. Unlike many baseball "fights" which involve just a lot of pushing and shoving, this one was real, with damage inflicted. It took six stitches to patch up my arm, for example.

I was not feeling so well on the train to Boston after that donnybrook. Lou Finney was sitting across from me and I said to him, "You know my neck is sore, I've got a headache, and I've got these knots on the back of my neck. I don't recall anybody hitting me." Finney said, "Clyde Milan was on your back the whole time you were after Myer, rabbit punching you in the neck. I picked him off of your back, took him over and sat him in our dugout." I later learned from Milan that when Finney deposited Clyde in the A's dugout he told him, "You sit right here old man. Someone is apt to kill you out there." Clyde, a great center fielder in his time and a teammate of Walter Johnson, was fifty at the time and he told me, "Always loved that Finney boy. He saved my life."

The melee lasted a good twenty minutes before the umpires and police could restore some semblance of order. Buddy Myer and I had a good laugh about our fracas the next time we saw each other and we remained friends with no hard feelings. Myer was an intense competitor who just lost his cool that day. Not that I am throwing stones, because I certainly lost my cool as well.

The next day in Boston Mr. Mack received, via the Red Sox front office, a telegram from the president of the American League, Will Harridge, stating that one William M. Werber was to be suspended for three days for his role in the fight in Washington. The Red Sox knew what the telegram said, but Mr. Mack, having already submitted his lineup to the umpires with yours truly at third base, stuck the telegram in his pocket without reading it. Of course, he pretty much knew what it said anyway. In the seventh inning, I hit what turned out to be a game-winning home run over the left field wall at Fenway Park. The Red Sox then protested the game because of the use of a suspended player, but they got nowhere. They had had the telegram since 10 am and failed to deliver it until game time. Further, they had no business knowing the contents of the message. Mr. Mack was a shrewd one.

Teammates often come to blows or near blows. One of the most comical incidents that I witnessed involved Dick Bartell and John Mize, teammates of mine in 1942 with the New York Giants. If there were ever two unalikes, it was Bartell and Mize. Both were great assets to a ballclub, Bartell for his aggressive spirit and Mize for his powerful bat. Bartell was a banty rooster, perhaps five-foot-nine and 160 pounds if you stretched him and weighed him wet. What he lacked in size he made up for in fight. He was rambunctious and into the ball game whether playing or gracing the bench. "Rowdy Richard," as he was called, played shortstop in the majors for eighteen years, six times batting over .300. He played for three pennant winners and got into enough scraps and fights to fill this entire chapter.

John Mize was not of the same mold. They called him "the Big Cat" for his size (six-foot-two and 215 pounds) and graceful moves. His arms were

Phlegmatic, powerful Johnny Mize sliding into home.

like the village blacksmith's. John's disposition was on the phlegmatic side and unless he had a bat in his hands facing the pitcher, he was mostly asleep. With that bat in his hands and the game on the line, he was a fearsome sight. A fine contact hitter despite his power (359 lifetime home runs and only 524 strikeouts), he always hit the ball hard somewhere.

During a very hot afternoon in the dog days of August, 1942, the Big Cat was playing first base for the Giants at the Polo Grounds and "Rowdy Richard," not in the lineup, was pacing the dugout and exhorting his teammates to do better. A routine grounder to shortstop Billy Jurges produced a low throw to first. It dribbled through Mize's feet and got about fifteen or twenty feet behind him. A normal amount of hustle would have held the runner to second base, but Mize just ambled after the ball and the runner went on to third. Fortunately, the next batter made the third out to end the inning.

Mize lumbered into the Giants' dugout and wearily picked up a towel to wipe the perspiration from his face. The feisty Bartell immediately accosted him, unleashing a plethora of personally directed oaths, including "If you don't want to play, get the hell out of there." John, with his face buried in the towel, indifferently waved him away. Angered by this casual attitude, Bartell, now with fist doubled, pushed himself into Mize's body. At that, Mize looked up from his towel, and pushing his forefinger against his thumb, said in a very tired voice, "Go sit down, Dick, or I'll pinch your head off." The absurdity of the episode brought a bunch of belly laughs from all of us within hearing distance. Mize and Bartell remained friends.

Speaking of Bartell, he took a lot of heat, unfairly in my judgment, for a play in the seventh game of the 1940 World Series. Bartell was playing shortstop for the Detroit Tigers against my Cincinnati Reds with the score 1-0 in favor of Detroit in the seventh inning. Bartell was a very heady ballplayer with a sense of awareness that comes with experience and intelligence. It was this awareness that led to considerable criticism. Frank McCormick of Cincinnati led off the bottom of the seventh with a double.

Although Frank was a fine ballplayer and great hitter, he was slow afoot and not always as aware of game situations as he should have been. The next batter, Jimmie Ripple, smacked a line-drive double off the wire screen in right field. Bruce Campbell was in right and had only an average arm. McCormick should have seen when the ball was hit that Campbell had no chance to catch it and that he could score easily, but for some reason he pulled up at third. The entire Cincinnati bench erupted and screamed at him, "Run, run, run." Bill McKechnie was coaching third and frantically waving McCormick home. Thirty-five thousand Reds' fans roared in unison for Frank to score. Given all that prompting, Frank got into motion again and did score the tying run.

In the meantime, Campbell had retrieved the ball and thrown it over the cutoff man, Charlie Gehringer, to Bartell at second base. Dick's awareness and reasoning led him to assume that McCormick would score easily on the double and that his responsibility was to receive the throw from Campbell and if possible try to tag out Ripple, representing the winning run, coming into second. As a result, Bartell did not check McCormick, thinking he would score easily, nor did any of his teammates tell him he had a play at the plate, or if they did, he could not hear them because of the crowd noise. The only one really at fault in this strange episode was McCormick. I do not think even Frank knew why he stopped at third.

Even teammates who are close friends can, in the heat of the moment, go after one another. It happened in a World Series to Paul Derringer and Ival Goodman, who were indeed good friends. Derringer was a great pitcher and an intense competitor who wanted to win at all costs but, with one exception, he never blamed his teammates for a loss. That one time came after the first game of the 1939 World Series against New York at Yankee Stadium. Derringer and Red Ruffing had hooked up in a pitching duel with the score tied, 1-1, going into the last of the ninth inning. With one out, Charlie Keller smacked a long fly ball near the right-center field bleachers which fell between right fielder Ival Goodman and center field-er Harry Craft for a triple. Goodman probably should have caught the ball but was bedeviled by the October shadows of Yankee Stadium and mis-played it. Bill Dickey then singled to win the game for the Yankees, 2-1. In the clubhouse immediately after the game Derringer was visibly upset. When he saw Goodman, he could not contain himself and popped off, "If you got no guts, get out of there. That was the most gutless effort I've ever seen." Derringer had pitched his heart out, allowing only four hits, but he was out of line. Goodman was a competitor, too, and you could not tell him he had no guts without consequences, so Ival threw a right hand at Derringer's jaw, right there in the clubhouse. Teammates immediately sep-arated the two and our manager, Bill McKechnie, quickly hollered, "Shut the doors. Don't let any sportswriters or anyone else in the door until we get this straightened out." Then he told Derringer and Goodman to shake hands and said, "If any news of this gets out of this clubhouse, it is going to cost someone $1,000." After about ten minutes, the doors were opened and the reporters admitted. Never a line appeared in print about the aborted fight. Goodman and Derringer eventually laughed it off and remained friends.

I have to report that I, too, once was involved in a fight with a team-mate. He was Babe Dahlgren, a pleasant and agreeable man, with an exceptional glove and a modest bat. Babe hailed from the Bay Area, had a solid twelve-year big-league career, and is best known for replacing Lou Gehrig at first base on May 2, 1939 when Lou ended his consecutive-game playing streak. In 1935, however, he was a rookie first baseman with my Boston Red Sox, up from the Pacific Coast League.

In the middle of the summer, the Red Sox lost some games that we should have won and tempers were short. One hot afternoon found Rube Walberg on the mound for us. Rube, though eccentric, had been a hurler of considerable talent for thirteen years with the Athletics and Red Sox. A ball was hit to Dahlgren that required Rube to cover first to receive the throw for the expected putout. Instead, Babe fielded the ball and managed to toss it squarely into the middle of Walberg's back because Rube had yet to turn to catch the throw. It was a dumb play on Dahlgren's part and I made the mistake of telling him so when we reached the Sox dugout at the end of the inning. He was as annoyed as I was and gave me his thoughts in what I considered strong language. In the dugout was a large tin bucket of Florida water and ice along with a sponge for wiping the sweat from your face. At that moment the sponge was in my hand and I shoved it into Babe's face. The next thing I felt was his fist against my jaw and my head rocked against the concrete wall of the dugout. My left caught him on the bridge of his nose and blood gushed out on his uniform and the dugout floor. At that juncture teammates separated us, to my great benefit. I had not known that Dahlgren had been an amateur boxer of some accomplishment in his native California.

Babe and I remained friends, but he was traded in 1936 and I did not hear from him again until he was playing for the Pittsburgh Pirates in 1944. He wrote me and asked that I straighten out some sportswriter who had questioned his response to my aggression back in 1936. I wrote the writer and told him that the fault was all mine and that if the fight had continued I would have taken a good licking, which of course was true. Never heard from Babe or the writer, though.

I really did not care for Leo Durocher. He represented everything I disliked in the game. He was famous for trying to intimidate the other team whenever he could, and he would have his pitchers throw at you. All that did was make the opposition mad and more intent on beating him. One day in Cincinnati when Durocher was managing the Dodgers he ordered his ace righthander Whitlow Wyatt to hit every man in our lineup—and he did. We beat the daylights out of Wyatt, scoring something like 23 runs off of him, but Durocher left him in the ballgame just to throw at us.

I did not say anything to anybody, but I made up my mind that if I ever got the chance I was going to lift Durocher's teeth right out of his mouth. The Dodgers were still in town the following day, a Sunday, and Durocher, who was then a player-manager, was at shortstop. I reached first base and got a big jump on a ground ball to second baseman Pete Coscarart. Durocher had to cover the bag and I went into second with my feet about belt high. I wanted to do him serious damage, to tell the truth. The next thing I know all the Reds players were gathered around me, laughing. I asked, "What happened?" I thought maybe Durocher had hit me in the head with the ball. Bill McKechnie said, "Well, you tried to kick him in the belly and your head came down before your feet did." I had knocked myself out at second base. I hit my head on the ground and never touched Durocher. He got the ball from Coscarart, stepped on the base and was gone before I got there.

Durocher irritated me and I irritated Durocher. When he was not playing, he coached third base, and, of course, I played third base. The last thing I would do at the start of an inning after warmups was to go over and kick the third base bag in toward the infield. Durocher would then come over from the coaching box after I had returned to my position and kick the bag toward the foul line. The advantage to either of us from all this kicking was infinitesimal, but that did not stop us from doing it. One day he kicked the bag two or three times and I told him, "You kick that bag one more time and I'm going to take you." He did not kick it anymore after that. If he had I would have gone after him. Can you imagine the headlines if a fight had broken out over kicking the third base bag? I never did take a swing at Durocher, but plenty of other ballplayers did.

6 BOYS WILL BE BOYS: SOME CHARACTERS FROM THE THIRTIES

The ballplayers of my day, 1930-1942, were not a sophisticated lot. They came from towns and villages, wide spots in the road like Ringgold, Texas; Ione, California, or Berwyn, Maryland, where I grew up. Very few had gone to college, but in most instances they came from good families, and had common sense and a capacity to learn. Their baseball skills had, for the most part, been developed on ball diamonds manufactured from pastures or vacant lots, and all could, in varying degrees, throw hard, run fast, and hit skillfully and for distance.

Big cities, large stadia, three-tiered movie houses and underground transportation that rattled and banged over long distances in a great hurry were intimidating and awe-inspiring to many of these young men from the country. They just laughed and took no offense at the city people who shoved and jostled to push their way onto the subway train. Even city kids were awestruck on their first trip to New York. Dario Lodigiani was another of the long line of Italian ballplayers from San Francisco. He was a small and slight second baseman and had been Joe DiMaggio's double play partner in junior high. He was in spring training with the Philadelphia A's in 1938, made the team and headed north with us from our training camp in Lake Charles, Louisiana.

After an exhibition game in Jersey City, New Jersey, several ballplayers decided at dinner to go into New York City to the movie and stage show at Radio City Music Hall. Dario asked if he could go along and he was most welcome since he was a jovial and lively sort. At the ticket window we were told that the only available seats were in the third balcony. We bought tickets, took the elevator to the third floor, and eased our way to our seats in the darkened theater. It was only a few minutes until the movie ended and the house lights came on. All was quiet in the third balcony until Dario had taken in his surroundings. When he did, he shouted, "Jeez! Lookit the size of this place. Ain't nuthin' like this in Frisco." The quiet broken, the third balcony erupted in laughter.

A year or two later, when I was with Cincinnati, we were in New Orleans for a spring exhibition game. Since New Orleans, then as now, was noted for its restaurants of quality, several of us decided to dine at the best. Antoine's was the choice, but it was dark in the lushly carpeted room and the menu was printed in French or maybe Creole, so the four Reds at the table asked for suggestions. Three of us ordered froglegs, crayfish, and jambalaya, respectively, but Billy Myers, our shortstop who hailed from Enola, Pennsylvania, was indecisive.

"The specialty of the house," suggested the patient waiter, "is Pompano en Papillotte."

"I'll take it," said Billy, adding to us, "You guys don't know how to order."

Our eyes had adjusted to the darkness somewhat by the time our meals were served, but the Pompano en Papillotte posed a problem for Myers. "How the hell do you eat this thing?" he asked. "Why you hold it with your fork, cut off pieces with your knife and eat it—like with catfish," we replied. When we later asked Myers how he had liked his fish, he said, "Lousy." His response was understandable. He had eaten the paper bag in which the pompano was cooked.

Ray Berres was a catcher who hailed from Kenosha, Wisconsin—dairy country—where he grew up among Swedes and Norwegians. He was one of those quiet guys you never knew was around, laughing a lot at other people's jokes but adding little of his own to a conversation. He drew a National League paycheck for eleven years but was never a first-string catcher. For his career he appeared in 561 games with a lifetime batting average of .216. Yet he was a good catcher with a decent-enough arm, savvy, and hustle. In 1942, Ray and I joined the New York Giants and became roommates. Ray was one of the best I had in baseball.

Most ballplayers of my day kept their hair cut short because most of the 154 games were played under a hot sun, causing your head to sweat profusely. It was easier to shower out the sweat and dirt if your hair was short. Ray was different. He maintained a luxuriant head of thick, wavy brown hair that was foreign to any hat away from the diamond. To say that Ray savored his head of hair is putting it mildly. We had played a double-header on a Sunday afternoon at the Polo Grounds to finish off a homestand and our train was to leave from Grand Central Station for the west at 10 PM. Ray and I had finished a leisurely dinner at a midtown restaurant and decided to walk the several blocks to the station to board our Pullman car. We had walked but a block when Ray let out a yelp as if someone had stabbed him in the back. He raked his hand over his thick head of hair and came up with the ugliest glob of foul smelling excrement I had ever witnessed. With the sickest expression ever seen on a human face, he moaned, "Eight million people in New York City and a pigeon unloads on me, dead center." Meanwhile, I was convulsed. Taking his handkerchief and wiping his head as best he could, he hurried along to our Pullman car and found the wash room. Ray filled a wash basin, dipped in his head and began to scrub with soap. Rinsed clean, he rubbed the fouled-up hair with his fingers, smelled the fingers, and filled up another wash basin to scub again. This must have gone on for an hour with me seeing the humor of it and Ray having no fun at all. "Listen, Bill," he said finally, in all seriousness, "None of the fellows knows anything about this. Can't we keep it that way?" Up to now I have, but that was fifty-eight years ago. I was reminded of it recently because it happened to my daughter Susie, on her right shoulder, eighty-six stories up on the observation deck of the Empire State Building. Guess lightning does strike twice.

All the train travel ballplayers endured in the 1930s and 1940s produced some engaging conversations. One I remember involved Rogers
Hornsby and was rather one-sided. It occurred in 1933, when the St. Louis
Browns and my Boston Red Sox happened to be on the same train west to
open a series in St. Louis. The two teams were in a battle for the cellar and
Browns' owner Phil Ball had recently fired manager Bill Killefer and
named the hardbitten Hornsby to replace him and try to inject some life
into the club. It is a long way from Boston to St. Louis in a Pullman and
midway through the trip Hornsby made his way into the Red Sox car and
took center stage. Hornsby was arguably the greatest righthanded hitter in
the history of the game, with a .358 lifetime batting average to prove it, so
we quickly gathered around him. As a lesser peon of the Red Sox who
thought he might learn a thing or two, I listened raptly for a couple of
hours while the master held the floor and talked hitting and, surprisingly
enough, eye care. He eschewed all movie houses—had never seen a
movie—bad for your eyes. On this he expounded for a full half-hour. He
believed reading was bad, as well, whether newspapers, magazines, or
books. He admonished us to get plenty of rest and to avoid whiskey. (He
did not say anything about avoiding racetracks, of which he was fond.)
Finally, having exhausted his fund of advice, Hornsby rose and departed. I
concluded that the man had exceptional eyesight, strong arms, wrists and
hands, superb coordination, a large ego, immense self-confidence, and little imagination. History also proved that he was a much better hitter than
he was a manager. The Browns still finished last that year.

All of those hours on trains also produced more than a few arguments.
A real doozy developed one day in 1940 as the Reds were rolling along the
rails to Cleveland for an exhibition game with the Indians. The discussion
began with how slaves before the Civil War crossed the Ohio River at
Cincinnati into free territory. Frank McCormick, Bucky Walters, and
Johnny Vander Meer argued that the Mason-Dixon Line ran down the
Ohio River to where it flowed into the Mississippi, and wherever slaves

from the South crossed that line they were free men. Ival Goodman, Paul Derringer, and Ernie Lombardi were willing to bet their season's pay that the Mason-Dixon Line had nothing to do with slavery, although crossing the Ohio River did. The contention became louder and more heated and the bets grew accordingly. By the time we reached Cleveland, over $500 was on the table, reduced to writing to record the bettors and amounts wagered. As the only college graduate on the club, I was asked to go to the public library in Cincinnati, conduct the necessary research and report back—without fee.

I did so at the first opportunity and provided the parties at interest with a written report. It turns out that the Mason-Dixon Line had nothing to do with slavery. William Penn and Lord Baltimore had received grants of land for colonization from King Charles II and were in dispute as to the boundary line between the two grants. Mason and Dixon were two surveyors sent by the king to settle the dispute. They began their survey in New Jersey near Trenton and laboriously headed west. They were forced to abandon their work east of Cumberland, Maryland, because of the increasing ferocity of attacks by hostile Indian tribes. The survey never got anywhere near the Ohio River.

My definitive report failed to quell the argument, which continued all summer, on and off. I am pretty certain that no money ever changed hands, and I doubt that any minds were changed or enlightened. Perhaps our Mason-Dixon argument did provide a useful diversion, however. The ballclub swept to the pennant and then defeated the Detroit Tigers in the World Series that year.

During my years in baseball I played on pennant winners, but I also saw the other side of life. It is not fun playing on a tail-end ballclub and I played on a few. The management is poor, the pitching is weak, and the players cannot quite run, field, or hit up to the competition. The days seem hotter and longer, the Pullmans never have air conditioning, the eggs are greasier, and the steaks tougher than wood siding. On top of all that, you don't get paid much on a bad ballclub, either.

The 1933 Boston Red Sox did not finish in last place, but the only reason is that the St. Louis Browns were worse. This was my first full year in the big leagues and there were not many bright spots. We won only 63 games, finishing 23 games under .500 and 34-1/2 games back of the pennant-winning Washington Senators. Still, that was a marked improvement for the Red Sox over their 1932 showing when they had won only 43 games and finished in the cellar, a whopping 64 games behind the first-place Yankees. The only bright spot that year was first baseman Dale Alexander, who through it all managed to hit .367 to lead the league in hitting.

The 1933 Red Sox were hardly household names, but had some memorable characters nonetheless. One was Smead Jolley, a hunk of Arkansas farm boy. He stood over six-foot-three and weighed about 210. He could hurt you quickly and easily if he wished, but the Lord fortunately makes these big guys good-humored. Smead was an outstanding hitter and had hit .397, .404, and .387 with the San Francisco Seals in the Pacific Coast League from 1927 through 1929. His statistics for the Seals in 1928 were of Ruthian proportions: 309 hits in 191 games, 143 runs scored, 52 doubles, 10 triples, 45 home runs, and 188 runs batted in.

Jolley had broken into the major leagues with the White Sox in 1930. By 1933 he was playing left field for us in Boston, in front of what is now called the Green Monster. In the early '30's the playing field ran level to within five or six feet of the wall and then sloped upward toward the fence. On top of the slope was a ledge and if you were agile enough and a good enough judge of a fly ball, you could run up the slope, balance on the ledge, and catch the ball to retire the batter. This area was known as "Duffy's Cliff," after Duffy Lewis, the onetime Boston left fielder who had mastered it. Smead had neither the speed nor agility nor judgment to handle that slope. Every day a coach would hit fungo after fungo to chase Jolley up that grassy slope to the wall. Then came the day that a batter in a game hit a ball to the wall that Jolley thought he might catch. He charged up the slope after it, but once on the ledge, lost his balance, tumbled over and plowed a furrow with his chin and nose into the slope coming down. Smead generally had an alibi for his fielding shortcomings, which were many, and his teammates in the dugout waited with anticipation to hear this one. When manager Marty McManus had finished unloading on him for "the clown act," Smead had his say: "Hell, you practiced me going up that bank but nobody practiced me coming down."

Although Jolley hit a solid .282 for us in 1933 and had a lifetime .305 average in four big-league seasons, by the following year he was back in the Coast League with the Hollywood Stars. He never made it to the major leagues again, although he averaged .366 in 16 minor league seasons.

Bob Seeds also was an outfielder with that '33 club, liked by everyone. He came from where the panhandles of Texas and Oklahoma run into each other and could have been called a hayseed until you got to know him better. Bob was lacking in proper early dental care and had a mouthful of prominent teeth. Some wag in the stands with a sharp eye and a loud mouth once yelled at Seeds, who was playing pepper, "Look at the guy with the air-cooled teeth. Only man I ever seen could eat corn on a cob through a picket fence."

Bob had a skill with his hands and a sharp penknife that I would not have believed had I not seen it myself. During spring training, Dusty Cooke, Bob, and I were walking the main thoroughfare of St. Petersburg, Florida, on a warm sunny day. Bob bought a paper bag of pecans from a street merchant and we sat on one of the numerous benches to enjoy them. Bob allowed from out of nowhere, "I'll betcha I can shell these pecans faster than you can eat 'em."

Ballplayers will bet on most anything and Cooke said he had five dollars that said Bob could not do it. Bob pulled his penknife from his back pocket, put the bag of pecans on the bench between his legs and, zip, zip, two halves of the pecan lay in Dusty's hand. It was no contest. Seeds had the bag of pecans shelled before Cooke could begin to eat them. Bob

Smead Jolley—great hit, little field.

accepted the five dollars, laughed, shelled some for me to enjoy at leisure, and we walked on down the street.

"Suitcase Bob," as the press called him, played nine years in the big leagues as a part-time outfielder for five teams and compiled a .277 lifetime average. He also played a key role for those great Newark Bears teams in the International League in 1937 and 1938.

The 1937 Bears are often regarded as the greatest team in minor league history, finishing with 109 victories and only 43 losses. They won the pennant by 25-1/2 games with players like Charlie Keller, Babe Dahlgren, Joe Gordon, George McQuinn, Willard Hershberger, who later become my teammate in Cincinnati before meeting his tragic end, and Buddy Rosar. Pitchers Atley Donald (19-2), Joe Beggs (21-4), Steve Sundra (15-4), and Vito Tamulis (18-6) combined for a 73-16 record.

Seeds hit .303 for the '37 Bears and led the team with 112 RBIs. The next year, however, he absolutely set the International League on fire, slugging 28 homers and driving in 95 runs in just the first 59 games of the season. On May 6 and 7, Bob had nothing less than one of the great two-day hitting rampages in baseball history. Against the Buffalo Bisons in Buffalo, he singled in his first at-bat, then followed with four consecutive home runs before singling again in his last trip to the plate. For the day he went 6 for 6 with 12 RBIs.

Incredibly, Bob hit home runs in his first two appearances the following day, making six homers in seven trips to the plate. After a base on balls, he knocked yet another home run in the sixth inning, his third of the day. In his last plate appearance he narrowly missed his fourth round tripper, when a smash deep into the stands in left curved foul at the last minute. The Bisons finally retired him with a disputed called third strike. For the two days he was 9 for 10 with seven home runs, 17 runs batted in, and 30 total bases. He clobbered five of his homers on 3-2 counts. The Giants purchased Bob's contract on June 24 for the not inconsiderable sum of $40,000. He hit .291 for the season and stayed with the team through

1940, before returning to the International League in 1941. Bob Seeds was a good man, a good ballplayer, and the world's fastest pecan sheller.

Zeke Bonura played nothing but first base in his seven-year major league career. He could hit, and had a lifetime .307 average to prove it. With the Chicago White Sox in 1936 and 1937 he carved out averages of .330 and .345 respectively. His fielding was another story, which probably explains his exclusive attachment to first base. He looked like a bouncing bear in his efforts to play first. Ponderous would describe his footwork.

Zeke's daddy owned a produce stand in a New Orleans market and there young Zeke lifted boxes of bananas and other produce when he was not off playing ball. He grew to a bit over six feet, weighed almost 220 pounds and was strong as a bull from lifting all that produce. The good Lord endowed "Old Zekie" with a great disposition and everyone liked him—everyone that is but Hank Greenberg.

Probably no one alive remembers why the usually affable Greenberg had it in for Zeke. In 1932, both played first base in the Texas League, Hank for Beaumont and Zeke for Dallas, and—the story goes—Greenberg got on Bonura every time the two teams played one another. Zeke shrugged it off and went about his business. If the other guy wished to be contentious, it was no concern of his. Zeke loved everybody, even the surly pitchers who threw at his head now and again.

Nonetheless, after a ballgame toward the end of the season, Hank apparently cornered Zeke and left him no choice but to defend himself. Greenberg was not exactly a midget, standing almost six-foot-four and weighing about 210 pounds, but evidently he had not hefted as many banana stalks as Bonura. If Zeke's teammates had not pulled Zeke off, it is questionable whether Greenberg would have ever made it to the American League.

In 1935, my Red Sox were involved in a tight ball game with Bonura's White Sox at Comiskey Park. Vern Kennedy was pitching for the Pale Hose with the score tied late in the game. Dusty Cooke was on first base and I occupied third with two out. Kennedy had a good move toward first and liked to throw over if a base runner took even a modest lead. So Kennedy took his stretch and threw quickly to Bonura at first. Zeke made a sweep tag with his glove hand. "Safe," bellowed the umpire.

Bonura sort of bounced up in the air, slapped his mitt, and with an encouraging "Come on, Vern ole boy," lobbed the ball in a high arc back toward the pitching mound. Taking all this in at third, I thought to myself, "If Kennedy throws over to first again and Zeke does his little dance and lobs the ball back, I'm gonna take off for home."

Sure enough, we had a repeat performance: Zeke slapping his glove, doing a little dance and lobbing the ball back to Kennedy. I had taken a healthy lead off third and was on my way home before the ball left Zeke's hand. I slid safely across with what turned out to be the winning run well before Kennedy could get the ball to home plate.

To get from the visitor's clubhouse to the playing field at Comiskey Park, you had to pass through the White Sox dugout. The next day Zeke was waiting for me as I came though the passage way. He grabbed me and wrapped his big arms around me, pinning my arms to my sides. I felt as if I were in the embrace of a gorilla and I pleaded, "Turn me loose, Zeke. You're cracking my ribs."

"That's just what I mean to do," he said. "You made ole Zeke look bad yesterday and Dykes fined me $250. You've gotta pay." But it was all in good fun and Zeke eventually turned me loose.

White Sox manager Jimmy Dykes traded Zeke to the Washington Senators before the 1938 season, much to the consternation of South Side fans who regarded him as a favorite. I was playing for the Athletics and stayed at my home in College Park, Maryland, when the A's played in Washington. The Senators graciously gave me permission to use the lot where their players parked their cars. As luck or misfortune would have it, depending on your point of view, one afternoon after an A's-Senators game I went to the lot to retrieve my car only to view an intriguing sight. There cozying up between the automobiles was none other than old Zeke and Thelma Griffith, daughter of Senator's owner Clark Griffith. Thelma later married Joe Haynes, a Senator's pitcher, but since both Zeke and she were single and it was broad daylight at five o'clock, it was only fun and games. I could not, however, let the opportunity pass. I startled them with, "Looky there, sucking up with the boss's daughter, eh? Wait till your teammates hear about this tomorrow." "Aw, come on, Bill, you wouldn't do that to your good friend," Zeke pleaded. Since he outweighed me by forty pounds or more, and since I had already felt the pressure of those vice-like arms, I allowed as how his indiscretion would remain between the two of us.

Clark Griffith was called "the Old Fox" for his wily ways. I do not know the reason, but Zeke only lasted one season in Washington before he was traded to the New York Giants. I do know that I never breathed a word about Zeke's little innocent romance in the parking lot.

About the time of Zeke's transfer to the Giants, Mr. Mack sold me to Cincinnati. When asked by a baseball writer what he thought about going to New York, Zeke put his foot in his mouth and stated for all the world that it was tough being sent down to the minors. Believe me, the National League in no way resembled the minor leagues and the Reds could not wait for Bonura to hit town.

The visitors' clubhouse in Crosley Field was down the left field line so opposing ballplayers exiting the clubhouse had to walk past the Reds' dugout, around home plate, to the visitors' dugout between home and first. The first time Zeke came to town the Reds were waiting for him and as he came into view gave him a blast like he had never heard before. He put both hands over his ears and made a mad dash to the Giants' dugout. He took it in good nature as was his wont. The Reds pitching staff worked him over pretty well, however, and he wielded a fruitless bat for the series.

It was twenty or so years after we both had played our last big league game that our paths crossed for the last time. The Grandstand Managers Club put on a testimonial dinner in Alexandria, Virginia, to honor Bucky

Harris. I suppose invitations were sent to all living former players ever to grace the Senators' roster. Zeke showed up, looking prosperous , and I was fortunate enough to be seated with him. We had a great visit, reliving old times. Zeke had an expensive van full of rabbit dogs waiting outside. They were in route to somewhere in the vicinity of Harrisburg, Pennsylvania, to run in field trials. The rabbit dogs, not Zeke.

Oscar "Ski" Melillo was a small, bandy-legged second baseman who played ten years for the St. Louis Browns and two more for the Red Sox. Ski was only five-foot-eight and 150 pounds but he had the uncanny knack of gobbling up everything hit to the right side of the infield. He was steady as the Rock of Gibraltar and possessed a strong arm. In 1933 with the Browns he handled 813 total chances and committed but seven errors. Although a banjo hitter without much power, he could place the ball and was always on base. He hit .306 in 1931 and .292 in 1933. Ski was my teammate with the Red Sox in 1935 and 1936 after he was traded over from the Browns. He was well-liked, good natured, and often the butt of player pranks.

Heinie Manush was considerably larger at six-foot-one and 200 pounds. He was a big strapping outfielder with a seventeen-year lifetime average of .330, earning him election to the Baseball Hall of Fame in 1964. He owned a batting title, hitting .378 for the Detroit Tigers in 1926. He hit .378 again in 1928, but missed another title by one point to Goose Goslin. Heinie was simply an exceptional hitter.

Manush and Melillo were buddies dating back to their days on the Browns. When Heinie joined the Red Sox in 1936 they naturally hung around together. Once, after an afternoon game in Sportsman's Park in St. Louis and dinner at the Chase Hotel, they decided to go downtown to a movie. Heinie was behind Ski at the ticket seller's window when a friendly cat rubbed against his leg. Heinie bought his ticket, absent-mindedly picked up the cat, rubbed its head a bit, and followed Ski into the darkened theater, still holding the cat. Then, due to some irrational prompting from one who shall remain nameless, Heinie tossed the cat onto the middle of Melillo's back. The cat, startled, reacted by sinking his claws into that back. Ski, feeling the pain of the claws and the weight of the cat, took off down the aisle screaming at the top of his lungs. The house lights went on while everybody stared and had a good laugh at Ski's expense. We eventually calmed poor Oscar down, and persuaded him to take a seat and enjoy the movie.

On another occasion Ski was the victim of a prank by Hank Johnson, another Red Sox teammate. Johnson, a pitcher, had spent seven years with the Yankees with indifferent success. He was one of four Yankees Tom Yawkey purchased in 1933, shortly after he bought the Beantowners. Hank was an easygoing Florida boy with a live fastball and sharp-breaking curve, but troubled by intermittent arm trouble, he won only 63 games in twelve years in the majors. One spring morning in 1935 Johnson drove from his home in Bradenton, where he lived all his seventy-six years, to the Red Sox spring training camp in Sarasota. All of a sudden, ahead of him in the road was an alligator, about three feet long, slowly crossing the highway. Any normal driver would have slowed or stopped and watched the reptile on its way, but not Hank. Instead, he jumped out of his car, outmaneuvered the critter, grabbed it, and popped it into the trunk of his car. When Johnson arrived at the Red Sox clubhouse in Sarasota, he put the 'gator in Melillo's locker, temporarily immobilized and covered by Ski's baseball shirt. Oscar soon arrived for the morning workout, reached for his shirt, only to find it hissing and snapping. The frightened second baseman tore out of the clubhouse and no amount of persuasion could get him to go back that day.

Johnson later removed the alligator from Oscar's locker and tethered it in a small courtyard in back of the clubhouse. Some of the players started to tease the gator by poking the knob end of a bat at its head. In a flash, it snapped a sizeable chunk out of that hard Hillerich & Bradsby ash bat. That sobered the guys considerably. It might well have been Melillo's hand.

Oscar Melillo—fine ballplayer in a small package.

As Melillo could have told you, ballplayers' "fun" can be rough and thoughtless, and the joke sometimes turns sour. One night in 1935, during spring training in Sarasota, Dusty Cooke, Dib Williams, and I were walking back to the Sarasota Terrace Hotel after going to a movie downtown. There was a wooded area between downtown and the hotel, and we saw a possum waddle out of the woods. Williams was from rural Arkansas and knew possums could not move very fast so he chased and caught it. He held the possum by the tail at arm's length to avoid its sharp teeth and carried it back to the hotel.

The Red Sox had a hardworking clubhouse boy named Johnny Orlando, and when we got back to the hotel, we checked to see if Johnny was in his room. He wasn't, so we got the key and put the possum in his bathroom. Then we unscrewed the lightbulbs in there. We staked out his room until Johnny came in about 10:30. He completely undressed before he went into the bathroom to brush his teeth. When he got in there, the possum bared his teeth in the dim light reflected from the other room, and hissed. Johnny, reacted as you might expect, finding a large toothy rodent in his dark bathroom. He raced to his door to flee, but Dusty Cooke had a hold of the knob from the other side, so he could not budge it. The transom was down, and Johnny tried to crawl through the transom, hollering the whole time, "It's a sewer rat, it's a sewer rat. It goes for my throat, it goes for my throat."

We realized that the joke may have gone too far, so we opened the door. Johnny, stark naked, bolted down the corridor as far as he could and squatted down beside a radiator at the end of the hall. The commotion caused several ballplayers in other rooms to open their doors to find a naked man running down the hall. By this time, we could see that Johnny was truly terrified and the joke was no longer funny. Once he learned about the prank, Johnny was a good sport, but we would never have pulled it if we'd known how frightened it would make him.

When fans talk about great catchers, Rollie Hemsley is generally not on the list. He is largely forgotten today, but I thought Rollie was a pretty fair receiver with a good arm, good speed, and considerable competitive instincts. Over a nineteen-year career, he caught 1,495 games and hit a solid .262. He was a friendly fellow, always wanting to talk when you came up to bat. He caught for the St. Louis Browns from 1934 through 1937, and maybe that was why he was so talkative. The Browns were the league's perennial doormats, and with the heat in St. Louis and the paucity of fans, perhaps he needed conversation to keep sane.

Rollie drank a bit after the game. You can smell the alcohol on a hot July or August day when a ballplayer begins to sweat, and there were afternoons when I caught the odor with Hemsley behind the plate. Or maybe it was the umpire.

Affable Rollie had a prankster's disposition and he planned a good one for his former Brown teammate Melillo when the Red Sox were in St. Louis for a series. Oscar was leaning against the batting cage waiting to take his swings when Hemsley came from the Brown's dugout for some typical pregame conversation. The previous evening Rollie had gone frogging, and inside his shirt he had a big bullfrog. As he began talking, he put his hand on Ski's shoulder. After a bit he gently substituted the bullfrog for his hand. When Oscar turned to say something to Rollie and saw that big, green bug-eyed amphibian staring at him he screamed loud enough to be heard about a mile away and tore from the batting cage, through the Red Sox dugout, to the relative safety of the clubhouse.

What prompts folks to do the things they do to other folks?

Another on the field prank involving animals took place when I was with the Athletics. Indian Bob Johnson, from Pryor, Oklahoma, was a good-hitting outfielder with power and a strong arm. He was good-natured to a fault and liked to have a little fun whenever the opportunity presented itself. Bob played left field for the A's and, as luck would have it, had a half-brother named Roy Johnson who played left field for the Boston Red Sox.

One evening we were playing a night game in Philadephia against the Red Sox when Bob noticed two bats—the flying kind—on the wall of the stadium. In those days fielders just left their gloves on the field when their team was at bat, so Bob took the two bats and placed them under Roy's glove in left field. When Bob came in at the end of the inning he alerted everyone in the A's dugout to watch for Roy's reaction when he picked up his glove. Roy was a high-strung, excitable sort of fellow and when he picked up his glove both bats flew up in his face. Roy took off across the outfield trying to get away from the creatures, throwing his glove up in the air with his hat flying off of his head. The A's dugout erupted in laughter at the spectacle in the outfield.

I knew Al Schacht as the third base coach for the 1935 Boston Red Sox. He claimed to have been a pitcher and the record shows that he put together a modest 14-10 record for the Washington Senators between 1919 and 1921. There he got to know Nick Altrock, a longtime Senators' coach

Rollie Hemsley, prankster at heart.

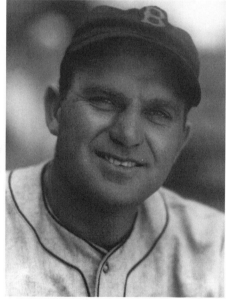

Heine Manush—the big Dutchman could play.

and resident clown. Schacht himself coached in the big leagues for fifteen years and, while doing so, developed a top-notch comedy act with Altrock. The act broke up when Altrock, in a skit, substituted a hard ball for a tennis ball and hit Al in the head and knocked him out. (This later became part of the plot of the movie, "Take Me Out To The Ball Game," in which the Frank Sinatra character beans the Gene Kelly character.)

From then on Al became a solo act, becoming known as "the Clown Prince of Baseball," and traveling to ballparks all over the country to put on his pantomine routines. He later ran a very successful restaurant in New York City, a couple of blocks from the Waldorf-Astoria Hotel, which for years was a popular meeting place for sports celebrities. He lived to be ninety-two years old.

In any event, in 1935 Al gave me the harrowing details of the time he was the shill in a "man with the gun" caper like the one Babe Ruth pulled on poor Ed Wells. This one happened during spring training in Orlando, Florida, when Al was with the Senators. His shepherd was Bucky Harris and Bucky had no difficulty persuading Al to buy the gin *and* the oranges. Schacht was young and single and eager. At the appointed time and place, there was the ringing of the doorbell, the maniac with the gun, and Harris screaming, "I'm shot, Al! Run for your life!" Oranges were all around Schacht's feet and, as he ran, he felt the thumps of the "bullets" in his back. But run he did, as fast as his feet would take him and for as long as his breath would last, with each step prepared to fall from the bullets in his back. Finally, he came to a street light, removed his coat and held it up to view the bullet holes. There were none and gradually he figured out that he had been had. The wadding from the blanks had hit him in the back and he didn't see a damn thing funny about it.

Schacht was a showman, with a flair for the dramatic, and his recital should have been recorded for posterity.

We pulled the same trick on Eddie Smith when I was with the Athletics, with hilarious but potentially dangerous results. Eddie would pitch ten years in the big leagues, mostly with the A's and the White Sox. His 73-113 won-loss record belies the fact that he was a pretty fair pitcher. He simply played for second-division teams and pitched in tough luck. For example, he was the losing pitcher in Bob Feller's 1-0 Opening Day no-hitter against the White Sox in 1940. He led the league with 20 losses in 1942, but his defeats included three 1-0 games, two 2-1 games and a 2-0 game. He was a youngster breaking in with the A's when he got roped into going to the gin and girls party during spring training in Louisiana. The house chosen was at the end of a heavily wooded dirt road. When the doorbell was rung and the aggrieved husband began to shoot, Eddie would have nowhere to go but back up the road whence he had come. Along the road, hidden in the woods were a few A's players with guns to help speed Eddie along as he flew past. Their additional shots made Eddie think that the man with the gun was at his heels.

The best laid plans, however, often go astray, and when the shooting at the house began, Eddie ran straight ahead through the trees rather than coming back up the road. He soon came to the Lake Charles River, so he dove in and swam a hundred yards, mostly under water, to the opposite bank. By the time he found his way back to the Lake Charles Hotel, it was early morning. For some reason, Eddie couldn't see the humor in the situation either.

Eric McNair played shortstop for fourteen years in the big leagues and for the first seven toiled for the Philadelphia Athletics. For some reason he was called "Boob" by his teammates, but there was no Boob in McNair. He was from the deep South—Meridian, Mississippi—and was good-natured, pleasant, and well-liked in addition to being a fine shortstop. His .274 lifetime batting average is evidence that he was a good all-round ballplayer.

Merritt Patrick Cain was also a Philadelphia A from the South—Macon, Georgia—and was best known as "Sugar Cain." In seven years in the American League he compiled a 53-60 won-loss record topped by a 15-11 record for the Browns and Chicago White Sox in 1936. His nickname was as misleading as McNair's. There was nothing sweet about Sugar Cain. He lacked the good nature that Eric possessed.

One early spring, the Athletics were at the Del Prado Hotel in Chicago's Southside for a series with the White Sox. The game that day had been called by the Sox because of the bitter cold. After sitting around the hotel all morning and through lunch, McNair, Cain, and several other players decided to don their raincoats and venture out to view the choppy water of frigid Lake Michigan. The wind was howling and the lake was turbulent, with waves smashing up against stone bulkheads. Standing there, Cain remarked that he would bet $100 that nobody would jump off that jetty into the lake. "Sugar," responded Boob, "I don't like you and I'm gonna take your $100. Can I take out my wallet and watch and take off my overcoat?" With that done and overcoat, watch, and wallet in the possession of Lou Finney, Eric jumped off the wall and into the frigid water of Lake Michigan. Almost before hitting the water he scrambled back on dry

Eric "Boob" McNair - a good
shortstop who was anything but.

Merritt "Sugar" Cain - he was
not all that sweet a guy.

land and ran hard for his room at the Del Prado to get out of his freezing clothes. Later at dinner, Eric, laughing in his quiet southern drawl, volunteered, "Paid the bell boy $2 to get my suit pressed and $1 to dry out and shine my shoes. Made $97 off ole Sugar." He didn't even catch cold.

There was a sad end to the life of this merry elf from Mississippi. In 1949, his wife died tragically from an illness and, overcome with grief, Eric took his own life. He was not yet 40 years old.

Although it should be fairly obvious that I was a leading perpetrator of pranks, I sometimes bore their brunt. My last year was 1942, when I played for the Giants. We stayed at the Coronado Hotel when we were in St. Louis, and the lack of air conditioning made sleeping a real problem. On this particular night, my roommate, Ray Berres, and I had managed to get to sleep by about ten when the phone rang, waking us both. It was, believe it or not, two coaches, Bubber Jonnard and Dolf Luque. Luque was from Cuba, where he was a legend, had pitched in the big leagues for twenty years, and was as sharp as they come. Jonnard had been a reserve catcher for four teams in parts of six years, but was also a very astute baseball man. In fact, manager Mel Ott delegated more responsibility to these two than most managers would have.

"Bill," came the voice over the phone, "this is Dolf and Bubber." Luque's "Bill," of course, came out as "Beel," and I knew who it was right away. "We got lotsa hot crawfish and cold beer and we're coming up." On this night, however, I was in no mood for company and told Dolf, "Don't come up here, Dolf. We're sound asleep." My protestations to the contrary, they beat on the door a couple of minutes later, and sure enough they were loaded with crawfish and cold beer. Bill Jurges had the connecting room and joined us. We soon wolfed down the crawfish and carefully wrapped the shell leavings in newspapers and stuffed them into our trash cans. I went into the bathroom to wash my face and hands to try to get some of the smell off me and, while I did, Dolf and Bubber took the opportunity to stuff shell hulks and leavings into my pillow case. They soon left and I went back to bed, trying to sleep on these smelly, rough shells. They soon soaked through the pillow case and into my face and hair. I had one bad dream after another all night and didn't know why. When morning finally came my face was all red and scratchy and I still didn't know what was wrong, so I went in to take a shower. While I was in the shower Jurges came over from his connecting room and threw the mess of crawfish remains on my back.

I did not see the humor, especially since we had a doubleheader to play that day. At breakfast I told Dolf that I wasn't going to play. Dolf said, "You play Bill, you play good, Bill." Well, I did play and managed to make an outstanding play in the field, nabbing a hot smash over third by Whitey Kurowski and throwing him out at first. When I went to the dugout Dolf said, "Bill, I told you you will play good. Only you could make that play."

Although Dolf's English was limited and his accent strong, he knew baseball in any language. He was an excellent coach and a great morale builder. I did get him back later in a minor way. He celebrated a birthday that summer and we had a little party for him and gave him some silly gifts. I bought him a tie and cut holes in it and sewed little bolts and screws and buttons onto it, put it into an expensive box and wrapped it with red ribbon. He took forever untying the ribbon, opening the box, and removing the tissue paper. When he finally saw the tie, he said, "My God, Bill. How I wear this? How I wear this?"

7 THE BEAST AND LEFTY

I was fortunate during my eleven seasons in the major leagues to play with many of the finest ballplayers ever to put on a uniform. Jimmie Foxx and Lefty Grove were two of the best. They were friends and helped provide me a lifetime of memories.

The Beast. Jimmie Foxx was my teammate with the Red Sox in 1936 and an American League opponent of mine for most of the 1930s. He was born on a farm on the Eastern Shore of Maryland, near the small town of Sudlersville in 1907. A great natural athlete, he starred in track, soccer, basketball, and baseball in high school and won the state 100-yard-dash competition yards ahead of his nearest competition.

When I was at Duke in 1929, Athletics scout Ira Thomas visited us to evaluate some of our baseball players. The varsity was coached by Thomas' old Athletics battery mate, Jack Coombs. Thomas had been a catcher of limited skill with the A's from 1909 through 1915. He possessed a pleasant personality and could really weave a yarn. In Coombs' apartment after a game on the Duke campus, Thomas spun one good tale after another to an rapt and gullible audience.

Thomas told us he traveled to Sudlersville to sign this country bumpkin whose fame as a high schooler and then as a catcher in the Eastern Shore League had piqued Connie Mack's interest. He'd gotten directions to the Foxx farm but the country roads were not marked and he got confused. He noted a powerfully built youngster plowing a field nearby, making his furrows straight and deep, and wondered at the lack of a mule or a horse. "Could you tell me how to get to the Foxx farm?" he asked.

The lad working the land picked up the plow with one hand and pointed it down the road. "You go down this road 'bout a quarter mile to a crossing, take a right and you see the farmhouse up the road a speck." According to Thomas, that was how he met young Jimmie Foxx.

The actual story of how Foxx signed with the Athletics was as interesting as Ira Thomas' yarn, but I didn't learn it for thirty years. I was hunting the Anchorage Farm on the Choptank River with Frank (Home Run) Baker one fall when Frank told me the true facts. Baker was managing Easton in the Eastern Shore League in the summer of 1924 and his catcher was sixteen-year-old Jimmie Foxx. Frank could see big league potential all over young Jimmie. He could run, throw, catch, and was strong as a bull at the plate, slamming drives over every fence in the league.

Frank took advantage of an off-day and traveled to Philadelphia where the Yankees were in town to play the Athletics. Frank had played with the Yankees from 1916 through 1922, and was on good terms with Yankee manager Miller Huggins. "Mr. Huggins," Frank said, "I've got a boy who can do it all right now. He can hit, run, field and throw with the best you've got and you can buy his contract for $2,500." Huggins, considered one of the most astute judges of baseball talent anywhere, inexplicably replied, "I don't think we can use him, Frank."

Baker took the dismissal quietly, and simply walked across Shibe Park to visit Connie Mack, his manager from 1908 through 1914, when he'd been a premier third baseman and a member of Mr. Mack's famed "$100,000 infield." Baker made his pitch, and Mr. Mack dispatched one of his scouts, Mike Brennan, to take a look. By the end of July, the Athletics had purchased Foxx from Easton for $2,500, with a provision that he not report until the end of the Shore League season. He traveled with the A's for the last month of the season, appearing in exhibition games. After the season he returned to Sudlersville to begin his senior year of high school.

The rest, as they say, is history. Foxx played for Mr. Mack until 1935, and was the star first baseman on the 1929, 1930, and 1931 World Championship teams, which rate among the greatest teams in baseball history. In 1932, he smashed 58 home runs, drove in 169, and compiled a .749 slugging percentage, all league-leading figures. His .364 batting average was just three points behind the league leader, Dale Alexander. Foxx would go on to win batting championships in 1933 and 1938, and led the league in home runs and runs batted in three times. He spent twenty years in the big leagues, finishing with 534 home runs, a lifetime .325 batting average, and a .609 slugging average, fourth all-time behind Ruth, Williams, and Gehrig. Mr. Mack always referred to Foxx as his gift from Home Run Baker.

No one hit the ball as far as Jimmie Foxx. He hit them over the roof in left field in Shibe Park, over the roof in Detroit's Navin Field, and out of sight everywhere else. His gargantuan blasts became commonplace and no one thought to put a tape measure to them. In 1936 in a game in Cleveland's League Park, he hit a ball against Willis Hudlin through the top of a large white oak tree that stood well outside of the ballpark. When he hit it, all of us on the Red Sox bench came out of the dugout to see where it would land. Dusty Cooke turned to me and said, "It's a damn lie."

It was 417 feet to the left field bleachers in League Park, the bleachers themselves ran up another hundred feet or so and on top of the bleachers stood a tall Lux Soap ad. Beyond the sign stood the tree. Foxx cleared all the man-made structures by a good distance.

Foxx stood six feet tall and weighed 195 pounds. He was a beautiful physical specimen, with muscular forearms, thick wrists, big thighs and calves, a flat belly and muscles bulging from his chest. He cut his shirt sleeves high, not out of showmanship but to give his big arms enough room, but the sight had a powerful effect on opposing pitchers.

Jimmie was a good-natured guy, smiling all the time, happy and full of fun. You could not make him mad. He did not always hustle, though. We played together in Fenway Park and I would always slide into second safe-ly on balls I hit off of the short left field wall there. Foxx would invariably pull up at first on drives off the wall. I would get on him about this and he would wave me off good naturedly, "Aw, Bill, I can't do that. I'm not as fast as you are."

Then near the end of the '36 season, the Yankees were in Boston and the annual Yankee-Red Sox field day was held preceding one of the games. It featured a 100-yard dash with a $100 prize for the winner. Cooke, Foxx, and I were running for the Red Sox, while Ben Chapman, Myril Hoag, and Jake Powell represented the Yankees. The starter, pistol in hand, began his count down—"on your mark, get set . . ."—but before he said "go," I jumped the gun and was several yards out when the pistol sounded. I fully expect-ed to hear a second shot for the false start, but hearing none, I burned a rag toward the finish for that $100. At about the 85-yard mark I could feel someone breathing on me and thought it was Chapman, who could run like the wind. But it was not Chapman. It was Foxx, and he steamed right on by. The guy who always protested "I ain't as fast as you" pocketed the hundred bucks.

Foxx made good money playing baseball, and he spent it about as fast as it came in. He wore expensive sports clothes, drove a big Pierce Arrow automobile, smoked the best cigars, and enjoyed the best whiskey. In the off-season, he was a moving target, always on the go someplace. Frank Baker later told me that he tried to counsel Foxx. "Come back to the Eastern Shore during the off season," he told him, "Take up your life among the people you know and understand and the people who know and understand you." Frank told me that Jimmie would listen, smile, and nod his head in agreement, but would never follow the friendly advice.

I last saw Foxx play in the summer of 1942, when I was with the Giants. He was playing for the Cubs and catching the second game of a doubleheader in Wrigley Field, bloated and out of shape. Wrigley, at times, presented a danger to hitters because of the white shirts in the center field

Jimmie Foxx - the unfailingly good-natured beast.

bleachers. A pitch could come out of those shirts and be on you before you could even duck. On this day, a ball from the Giants pitcher turned the bill of Foxx's cap around. Jimmie had not seen the ball at all. On my next trip to the plate, I spoke to Foxx, who was still catching, "Why don't you get the hell out of here. You couldn't even see that pitch your last time at bat." He giggled, as always in his good-natured way, "Heh, heh, heh. A guy's gotta eat, doesn't he?"

I saw Foxx a number of years later he came to Washington to visit Marcus Chaconas, who had played with him on Baker's Eastern Shore League team. I had played with Chaconas as a teenager on the Georgetown A.C. team, so Marcus called, told me Jimmie was in town and asked me to play golf with them at the Columbia Country Club. They were both good guys, kindred spirits, and I readily agreed. When I saw Foxx, he looked like hell. His head seemed swollen and his teeth neglected, but he had that same sweet disposition. We had a fine time.

Foxx had some rough years and died too soon, on July 21, 1967, three months before his sixtieth birthday. He was without funds. With that constitution and personality he should have lived to be a hundred.

Robert Moses Grove, Mackerel, and My Big Toe. Lefty Grove is considered by many to be the greatest lefthanded pitcher in history. I was fortunate enough to be his teammate with the Boston Red Sox in 1934, 1935, and 1936. I admired his toughness and his grit and tenacity on the mound, and I enjoyed his company off it. I have often said that if I had one game I had to win, I would send Lefty Grove to the mound to win it.

He was a mountain man from Lonaconing, Maryland. A's scout Ira Thomas signed Grove, and told another apocyphal story about the occasion. Thomas found the Grove home in Lonaconing at almost dusk. He knocked on the door and was greeted by Grove's mother, who told him that her son was squirrel hunting but would be coming down the railroad right-of-way towards home "any time now."

Thomas elected to stroll up the rail tracks, and soon saw the angular Grove approaching with squirrels swinging dead, their tails fastened under his belt. Introductions over, Thomas asked where Grove's gun was. "Don't use no gun," was Lefty's response. "I kill 'em with rocks." Noting the incredulity on Thomas's face, Lefty took from his coat pocket a large smooth stone and threw a bullet with his right arm, busting a glass insulator on a telephone pole sixty feet away. Said the thoroughly astounded Thomas, "But I was told you were a lefthander." "Am," said Lefty, "but if I throwed at 'em left-handed I'd tear 'em all up."

I became teammates and friends with Lefty in the spring of 1934, when Connie Mack, to make ends meet in the depths of the Great Depression, sent Grove to the Red Sox for $125,000. Lefty had pitched nine spectacular years for the Athletics and had won 20 or more games the last seven seasons. During the A's pennant winning years of 1929, 1930, and 1931, Lefty had posted incomparable records of 20-6, 28-5 and 31-4. He had followed those years with 25- and 24-win years in 1932 and 1933, so his sale to the Red Sox was front-page news.

With all that hype, Lefty arrived at Sarasota, Florida, for spring training in 1934 with a very sore left shoulder that left him unable to throw without excruciating pain. He ran a lot to get his legs in shape, but he just could not throw. Finally one day he said to me, "I'm no good. I'm going on home." And sure enough, Lefty packed his bags and got on a train to head for his Maryland mountains. Phil Troy, the traveling secretary of the Red Sox, intercepted him and, after much persuasion, talked Grove into going to Boston instead for a complete physical examination. It was discovered that Lefty had impacted, infected, wisdom teeth. Once they were extracted, the pain in Lefty's shoulder subsided.

Grove had hardly thrown at all in spring training, but his legs were in shape so manager Bucky Harris started him in a game against the Tigers in Detroit early in the season. About the fourth or fifth inning Lefty struck a batter out and our catcher, Rick Ferrell, threw to me to start the ball

Lefty Grove - Ole Mose sure hated to lose!

around the horn. I immediately noticed blood on the ball. Instead of throwing to our shortstop, Lyn Lary, I walked the ball in to Lefty and said, "Where did this blood come from?" Then I saw that the inside of his middle finger was mostly raw meat. "Lefty," I said, "You can't pitch with a finger like that. You need to call it quits for the day." "Gimmie the damn ball and get your ass back to third," was Lefty's response. So I gave him the ball and back to third I went. He continued to pitch in what must have been intense pain. It was as great an exhibition of courage and intestinal fortitude as I ever saw on a baseball diamond.

Lefty did not like to lose, and, of course, he did not lose very much. If he did drop a tough ballgame, it was best to stay away from him afterward in the clubhouse. He was really hard on himself, but despite the stories, I never saw him blame a teammate for a poor play. Once I saw him come into the clubhouse after losing and grab his baseball shirt on either side and yank hard. There were several pops and buttons flew off in all directions and then rained on the floor. By the next day, though, he was fine.

The press was not too partial to Lefty because he did not make himself available. He liked his solitude and was not particularly sociable. If he was sitting in a hotel lobby and a sportswriter came up to talk to him, he would as like as not get up and leave. If cornered he was likely to be curt or sarcastic. I guess you could say Lefty was on the taciturn side. He thought his job was to win ballgames, not curry favor with anyone.

Even so, I liked Lefty and he liked me. We became good friends and would eat at each other's houses during the season and fish together during spring training. One night when we were having corn on the cob at his house in Boston, he demonstrated a very unusual but practical way to eat the corn. He took a slice of bread and buttered it thoroughly. Then he took the cob of corn and twisted it around in the bread. That method may not have been practiced in polite society, but it certainly beat having the butter from your knife run all over the place.

In the spring the mackerel would be running under the great bridge that spans the bay from Sarasota, Florida, over to Lido Beach. Lefty and I would be there by seven in the morning and catch them by the bushel with Johnson Silver minnows. Then we would take them back to the hotel in Sarasota where one of the cooks would fry them up for us for breakfast.

Johnny Cooney and his wife often came out to cast for mackerel on that bridge as well. Johnny played major league baseball for twenty years, first as a pitcher with the Boston Braves and then as an outfielder with the Dodgers and Braves. Mrs. Cooney was left-handed and she cast sidearm. Johnny used to remonstrate with her all the time, telling her, "Cast that line overhand, you're gonna hook somebody sometime. Cast overhand." There was a man called Kingfish who was responsible for working the drawbridge. One morning Lefty and I were a little late getting out to the bridge, and as we were walking out, here came Mrs. Cooney and Johnny—and Kingfish with one of those Johnson Silver Minnows stuck in his ear. The Cooneys were taking him to the hospital to get it removed. Johnny had a face as long as the Washington Monument. I said, "What happened, John?" He said, "I knowed it. I knowed she was gonna do it all the time. I been a-tellin' her. Now she's gone and done it." And the three of them went off to the hospital while Lefty and I had a good chuckle over the Kingfish's misfortune.

Although Lefty Grove and I were teammates for only three years, he was responsible—indirectly and unintentionally—for my preparing myself for life after baseball. It happened this way: Early in the 1934 season, Lefty struggled on the mound because he was still weak from his infection. His arm was not yet completely sound and he was having serious blister problems. He just was not himself. He would pitch four or five innings, get knocked around, and Bucky Harris would take him out. When Lefty walked to the dugout after getting pulled, all the guys on the bench would move away from the water bucket, because Lefty would invariably give it a swift kick with the side of his foot, sending water and ice flying everywhere and giving anyone nearby an unwanted shower.

Now, I sometimes had a temper on a baseball field as well, and late in the season I came off the field steaming about something and hauled off and kicked that water bucket as hard as I could. What I didn't know was that Doc Woods had gotten tired of Lefty's busting up these tin buckets and spewing ice and water all over the place. He had gone out and gotten a big bucket with iron bands riveted to it. When it was filled with water and ice it had a substantial mass, and when I kicked it, it didn't move. Not only had the bucket been replaced, but I had not been observant enough of Grove's technique. He always kicked the bucket with the side of his foot, I later learned, thus preserving his toes, while I went at it toe on. I fractured the big toe on my right foot, and that water-bucket injury caused me a great deal of pain and discomfort the rest of my days in baseball.

When this happened I was twenty-six years old and nearing the end of my second full big-league season. My batting average was way up among the league leaders—Gehrig, Gehringer, Manush, and Simmons—I was leading the league in stolen bases, and on my way to scoring 129 runs. Not too long before, nobody less than Ed Barrow, the long time secretary and general manager of the Yankees, had called me the best player in the American League. Even with a broken toe, I did not want to leave the line-up. I had told some folks that I was going to steal 40 bases and I guess my pride got the best of me. I played in 152 games that year, hit .321 and did end up stealing 40 bases to lead the league.

I finished the year in considerable pain, but thought that since I was young the toe would heal over the winter, so I didn't seek any special medical treatment. But my toe got worse because of a calcium block and bone spur that formed around the joint. I was in so much pain that I could not sit still to play bridge or go to a movie. The trainer carried a diathermy machine, which I used before every ballgame in 1935. The toe affected my play, although I did manage to lead the league in stolen bases again, this time with 29.

That fall I went to Johns Hopkins Hospital in Baltimore and saw Dr. George Bennett who was one of the leading orthopedists in the country. He told me, "If you have this operated on, I can't guarantee that you'll play again, but if you don't have it operated on, I guarantee that you won't play again." So I had the toe operated on. Dr. Bennett told me after the surgery, "This toe is going to continue to bother you because it won't stand the pounding. You drive off it when you run and when you hit. When you get through playing baseball you're going to have to have it operated on again."

Dr. Bennett was right. I played seven more years, but in pain all the time. I babied it the best I could with foam rubber in my shoe. The groundskeeper in Cincinnati even tried to help by always putting extra dirt around third base to give me some padding. But that toe was a constant problem for me from the day I kicked the water bucket in Boston in a fit of anger. It was certainly a contributing factor to my quitting baseball after the 1942 season. And Dr. Bennett was correct, I did need another surgery after baseball so that I could hunt, fish, play golf, and lead a normal life.

I never blamed anybody but myself for my toe problems, and I actually came to look at it as a good break, pardon the pun. With that toe, I did not know how long I would be able to stay in baseball and, with a wife and two children to worry about, it forced me to begin planning for life after baseball. As a result, when I left the game after 1942, I was ready to step into the insurance business full-time. If I had not emulated Lefty Grove and kicked the water bucket, who knows where I would have ended up.

8 THE FANS: THE GOOD, THE BAD, AND THE JUST PLAIN RUDE

My first memorable experience with the fickle nature of baseball fans came in 1933, my first year as a regular in the big leagues. I took over at shortstop for the Red Sox after they purchased me from the Yankees, and I took pride in playing with all-out hustle. Early in the year I made what I thought was an exceptional leaping, twisting catch of a Texas League pop-up. I then threw wildly to first, trying to double the runner. I was booed roundly by the Boston faithful. I ended up making three more errors that afternoon, all in similar situations. Each time I was razzed unmercifully, although I was giving everything I had on each play.

After the game I was very dejected. I sat in front of my locker and cried like a baby. I had had a bad day, but I felt that because I had tried my best the fans' reaction was unjust. My emotions just overpowered me and I resolved then that I would no longer let the fans get to me. I would simply not allow myself to get too down or too up because of the whims of the fans. A baseball season is a marathon and I knew there would be many highs and lows. I played the rest of my time in baseball that way, and it was a very good approach for my own mental health.

Back in the '30s, baseball so dominated the sports scene that almost all men had grown up with the sport and knew it quite well. Perhaps because they had played and were envious of those few who were good enough to make the big leagues, they expected a high level of hustle and skill and were intolerant of anything less. Fans were naturally quite partisan, too, and could be rough on the opposition. I sometimes thought spectators, whether hometown or opposition, were too rough on us.

One rainy spring afternoon in 1942, I found myself sitting over breakfast with several of my Giants teammates in a hotel coffee shop in Wichita, Kansas. We were barnstorming north with the Cleveland Indians and it was apparent that the rains would wash out our afternoon game. I was with Carl Hubbell, Hank Leiber, and Hal Schumacher, and we had in front of us an article in *The Saturday Evening Post* by noted sportswriter Tom Meany and Phil Rizzuto, entitled, "They Made Me a Big League Ballplayer." Rizzuto had broken in with the Yankees the previous year and, standing all of five-foor-six and weighing maybe 150 pounds, had hit .307 in 133 games. We were skeptical to say the least that anyone had "made" Phil a big leaguer.

Our talk turned to boorish fan behavior, and I had the idea that we might be able to put together an article that painted a picture of a ballplayer's view of fans. I solicited advice from Carl, Hank, and Hal and then, with a long afternoon to while away, retired to my room and proceeded to pen a lengthy exposition on the topic. I sent it to *The Saturday Evening Post* and they readily paid me $1,000 for it.

The article was published in the July 25, 1942, issue and was entitled "Ballplayer Boos Back," by Bill Werber as told to Harold Parrott. Not only did the magazine come up with an attention-grabbing title, it took considerable license with the substance of what I had to say, accentuating the negative. I'd had some unhappy run-ins, but I had also received some wonderful kindnesses from the public as well.

Surprisingly, perhaps, the bulk of the fans I heard from—and I received an avalanche of letters—were very supportive. They agreed that some fans were unnecessarily critical and abusive and did not mind my pointing that out. I found that the vast majority of folks attending a professional baseball game simply wanted to be entertained by excellent play and wanted their team to win, not necessarily in that order.

The best fans that I can recall in my thirteen years in the game were in

Cincinnati, where I played from 1939 through 1941. Of course, we had all the ingredients for a close relationship with the community during those years: a hustling, winning ballclub; a ballpark (Crosley Field), which provided a feeling of intimacy between fans and players, and a population financially able to fill the seats. The Queen City was simply a great baseball town, with its professional roots running all the way back to the 1869 Red Stockings of Harry Wright.

The 1939 Reds were the best defensive club in baseball. Our games were played in an hour and forty-five minutes and the pennant race with the Cardinals was neck-and-neck throughout the season. We played before full houses and fan support was intense. One day I stopped for gas on my way to Crosley Field. When the young man pumping the gas came to the the car window to get paid, he recognized me as a Reds player. With my money in his hands, he dropped to his knees beside the car door, closed his eyes and, looking heavenward, prayed in all solemnity, "Please God, let the Reds win today."

My doorbell rang one morning early in that 1939 season, when it already looked like the Reds might bring Cincinnati its first pennant since the 1919 Black Sox scandal. A pleasant-faced gentleman stood at the door with about the largest fruit basket I ever saw. "I'm Frank Glade," he said, extending his hand. "I work for the Kroger Grocery Company and I admire the way you play." It turned out that he was the director of personnel for Kroger. He had nothing in mind but extending the good will of the people of Cincinnati and making me feel welcome. From time to time he would show up for a very brief visit, never obtrusive and usually with a small gift. Until he died long after I retired from baseball, Frank would send a Christmas card with a note every year.

That spring of 1939, we rented a house on Neeb Road, just a block from the twelfth green of the Western Hills Country Club. Across the street was a fourteen-acre estate with a large home not visible to us, which belonged to a man named David Hedges Willey. Mr. Willey, I learned later, was the owner of a big lumber company and was the largest manufacturer of over-the-head garage doors east of the Mississippi River. His wife, Nell Willey, was as devout a Christian as her husband was rich. We later learned that after we moved in she said to her husband, "A new family has moved into the community and our Christian duty is to call upon them."

David Willey responded very directly: "I know. Damn dumb ballplayer. I ain't going." Nonetheless, several days later Mrs. Willey called with her husband in tow, and from that moment, he became a fan like no other. The Willey Lumber Company had, as a civic responsibility, leased a box at Crosley Field, but thereafter it was more often than not occupied by Mr. Willey, his binoculars, and his guests. And after dinner, he could be sighted walking across to our house to review the mechanics of my play that day.

"Son," he'd begin, "I had the glasses on you today and the reason you didn't get any hits was due to a change in your stance." Then he would diagram for me how my feet were fixed when I was hitting well and how they were that day. He was often right and I loved listening to him. When I hit a home run, his cook would make us a gallon of peach ice cream, which the old gentleman would deliver—and help us eat. I was blessed with his friendship until he passed away.

Then there was Jack Schiff, president and CEO of Cincinnati Financial, a large and wealthy conglomerate. Jack appeared one day with a box of chocolates under his arm, no objective other than a friendly gesture and to express appreciation for my efforts on the playing field. We remained fast friends until Jack passed away in 1998 with our roles reversed: I became an ardent admirer of his.

Three more baseball fans whom I remember were enormously successful businessmen in New York City. Gene Black headed the Chase National Bank and was later president of the World Bank. Jonas Anderson was his righthand man and possibly the smarter of the two. The third was David Marx, who manufactured and distributed a variety of toys nationwide. These were not rabid fans who hollered for any one team, but they maintained boxes for their own entertainment and to host customers or clients. On the days, or nights, when they personally attended, they quietly observed and munched on a bag of peanuts. It would be my guess that not a one of the three had ever played youth, high-school or college baseball, yet all three were quite knowledgeable. So what was their attraction to the sweaty, rough-hewn professional baseball player?

For my connection to these financial movers and shakers you have to go back to the 1928-1929 academic year at Duke when the stock market crashed and men were jumping out of windows in New York City. Kids were leaving college because their parents could no longer support them there. Two of my classmates at Duke, Bob Hatcher and W.J. Hobbs, did not want to leave school, so they put their heads together and developed a black-face act, with spats, white pants and brown coat, white gloves, and a derby hat. They performed some soft shoe and sang songs, and were very good at it—so good that there were more demands on their time at fraternity parties than their academic standing could afford. As a result, Messrs. Hatcher and Hobbs were summoned to the office of the Dean of Students, William Hane Wannamaker, and told to abandon their entertainment endeavors or leave the university as academic failures. From there, I am not sure by what paths, Bob Hatcher became head of the bond department at the Chase National Bank, and W.J. Hobbs became president of Coca-Cola.

By the time I was playing third base for the World Champion Cincinnati Reds, Hatcher was on a first-name basis with Messrs. Black, and Anderson. On a trip to New York, Bob asked if I could come down to the bank for lunch and bring Ernie Lombardi, Paul Derringer, Bucky Walters, or manager Bill McKechnie to meet Anderson and Black. (Bob was circumspect about whom to invite, because he knew that some of my teammates, although adept at running, fielding and throwing, lacked equal skills at the dinner table.)

So I brought along a couple of ballplayers to invade the habitat of the bulls of Wall Street. It was a delightful lunch, without a word spoken about finance. Rather, our hosts peppered us with questions about baseball, and after the meal we all got in a cab for Ebbets Field and played the Dodgers. The bankers enlarged their baseball vocabulary and learned some "inside stuff" to share with their financial peers. We ballplayers had a chance to dine off linen tablecloths using clear crystal, polished silver, and fine china.

In New York, the Reds often ate at Dinty Moore's, then a popular restaurant. The food was good, and Dinty was an old-time Irishman who loved to talk to us about the game. Not only that, he had good cold beer on tap, served in frosted glasses, and sometimes he would get carried away, wave his hand and announce, "This one's on the house." When it was hot and humid at the Polo Grounds, we welcomed a cold beer and good meal at Dinty Moore's.

David Marx always seemed to be there, too—whether for the food or the conversation I'm not sure. Normally, he would get a chair at our table to rub elbows with the ballplayers and Dinty. It made for conviviality and a pleasant dinner and usually ended with Mr. Marx asking us if we would like to see a show. He would call the box office at the theater and we would wind up with seats in the second or third row for shows like "Carousel" or "Panama Hattie" that had been sold out for months.

It wasn't all roses, of course. We had our share of unpleasant encounters with fans—usually those in other cities. Dodger fans were good examples of pure cussedness in their support of "dem Bums." Visiting teams usually stayed at the better hotels in Manhattan and took the subway to Brooklyn for games. There was a magazine stand next to the subway exit we used to get to Ebbets Field, and as we reached street level, the proprietor would greet us with, "Ya' stinkin' bums, you'll lose today." The two blocks to the ballpark provided much the same invective from Brooklyn's general populace.

At Ebbets Field, the visitors' dressing room was under the stands on the first base side, and our dugout was across the field, so we couldn't just emerge onto our bench. Once we'd dressed, we had to get to the field by walking about thirty feet between barriers of iron bars spaced about a foot apart in either side. On these iron bars, like so many gorillas in a zoo, hung the denizens of Brooklyn, yelling and cursing and spitting, "Ya' stinking bums, we'll git youse today." Faced with that we were ready to take the Dodgers apart by the time we got to our dugout.

The animosity continued throughout the ballgame. On doubleheader days these everyday citizens would bring to the ballpark brown-bag snacks of hard-boiled eggs, tomatoes, bananas, and oranges. They would then use the sodden residue as projectiles. One afternoon in the second game, I ran over to the stands after of a high foul ball. It came down in the lower box seats five or six feet beyond my farthest reach, but as I stretched into the crowd a large wet brown bag sailed by my glove hand, splashing on the ground behind me.

"Interference! Interference!" I yelled at umpire Babe Pinelli, who was on top of the play. In a very quiet and friendly manner, Pinelli responded, "No, Bill, If you coulda caught it, I woulda called it, but that ball was fifteen feet up in the stands." I am not sure who picked up the garbage from the splattered bags, but it must have been a big job after every game.

Brooklyn fans were especially rough if the Dodgers were contending and playing another contender. One day late in the 1939 season, George Magerkurth, a big, burly, tobacco-chewing umpire, had a game where most of his decisions seemed to favor the visitors, my hated, league-leading Cincinnati Reds. When the last Dodger batter was retired in the bottom of the ninth, Magerkurth walked to the mound to retrieve the resin bag. He was suddenly attacked by half a dozen enraged Brooklynites, thrown to the ground, and pummeled. You've probably seen the famous photo of the umpire on the ground being pounded by one of his attackers. I had sauntered over to the box seats to visit with an old Duke classmate I had not seen in years. I turned to see Magerkurth being pounded. I ran over and with the help of a teammate pulled several of the thugs off until the police arrived. Just another day in the life of an umpire at Ebbets Field.

Normally, we paid no attention to whatever verbal abuse fans hurled our way. There was not too much really bad stuff and we figured taking some razzing came with the territory. It was a small price to pay for the short hours of work, comparatively high pay, and making a living at a boys' game most of us would have played for nothing. Once in a while though, they get you on a bad day. The kids are home sick, you are in a batting slump, it's hot as hell, and this wise guy has a box seat with his nose stuck in your dugout. He singles you out: "You stink. You should be ashamed to take pay the way you play. Where'd you ever learn to play ball?" You're steaming. And then it gets worse. It becomes personal.

Such a day arrived for me at old Griffith Stadium during a double-header between the Senators and my Red Sox. Our dugout was on the third base side where I was playing. The box seats extended beyond the dugout, and this leatherneck had a seat that put him virtually in it. After we were retired in the first, I ran out to take my position. This yokel gave me a blast: "Just a lousy bum from Berwyn." So he knew my background. I was raised just ten miles from Griffith Stadium.

That was the kindest thing he said. Cal Hubbard was umpiring the bases and he was a tough one, big and rugged. He had played tackle for the Green Bay Packers well enough to earn entry into the Pro Football Hall of Fame. Toward the end of the first game, I asked him, "Cal, you been listening to that loudmouth over there?"

"Yeah, I've heard him."

"Between games if I sort of take care of him, will you report me?"

"Do what you want, Bill. I will not have seen or heard a thing."

When the first game ended and our dugout cleared, I walked to the boxes and in my most pleasant manner addressed my constant heckler, "Look friend, you appear to be a decent enough chap. Why don't we talk about our problem here in the dugout. I've got another ballgame to play."

There was no response. He just turned his head and looked toward the left field bleachers. I tried again, just as politely and well-mannered as I knew how. Same response.

In the dugout was the usual large bucket of water, ice, and Florida water that the players used to sponge their faces and get the sweat off their hands. Toward game's end, it could get kind of muddy. I went down the steps, picked up that pail of dirty water, walked back to the end of the dugout, and dumped it over the heckler's head. The second game was played in relative peace and quiet. Hubbard never did ask me what I did.

I played third base for the Red Sox from 1933 through 1936, when I was traded to the Athletics for their third baseman, Pinky Higgins. On my first appearance at the plate back at Fenway, the fans gave me a nice round of applause. Not so a well-groomed young man in a white coat sitting on the front seat of the boxes nearest the A's dugout between third and home. In well modulated and cultured Boston tones he volunteered, "No wonder they traded you off. You stink." He didn't have to be loud for me to hear him because he was only ten feet or so from the crushed black cinder walkway that led from the bat rack to the on deck circle.

Each of the first three times I walked up to hit, this patron had some quiet but ugly and cutting remarks for me. Before my last time at bat I told the bat boy to take my bats up to the on deck circle and I would follow him. On the way, I stopped, picked up a double handful of the black crushed cinders and deposited them down the front of the white coat of the gentleman in the box seat.

After the game was over, the A's clubhouse boy came over to tell me that a man at the entrance would like to speak to me. It was the man in the white coat. He said he wished to apologize, that had not meant to offend, that he was a disabled war veteran at a facility near Boston, and that a group were in attendance as guests of the Red Sox. You just never know.

Although the ball fans of the '30s were not normally meanspirited, they certainly could be. In 1934, I watched the Boston fans mistreat the great Babe Ruth in a way that saddens me still. I was with the Red Sox and we were playing the Yankees on a Sunday afternoon before about 30,000 folks crammed into Fenway Park. The way the crowd acted I seriously doubt if any had attended church that morning.

Ruth was in his last year with the Yankees and, at 39, was just about through as a ballplayer. On this day he struck out twice and popped out in his first three trips to the plate, earning the lusty boos of the Red Sox faithful. Then, in the seventh inning, I hit a sinking line drive that he came lumbering in for. He tried to make the catch a little below his knees, but the ball glanced off his glove and rolled all the way to the wall. I easily made it to third, giving Babe a three-base error. The fans booed him for that and, even worse, laughed at him.

To top it off, when Ruth next came to the plate he struck out again, this time on three pitches. The boos and jeers just swelled up until they practically tore the roof off. It was a sad day for baseball, and not just because the game's greatest star was near the end of the line.

When I joined Cincinnati in the spring of '39 I saw how jeering and booing could sap the confidence of a ballplayer and even affect a team's pennant aspirations. My first appearance in a Reds uniform was in a spring-training game in Tampa, Florida, against the Red Sox on a Sunday afternoon. Before the game, the Reds shortstop, Billy Myers, came over and, behind his glove, asked me, "How are you on pop flies?"

I told him, "I can catch anything I can get to."

"Good," he said, "Take any you can get to." He said the sun bothered him, but I was suspicious, since there really was no problem in Tampa.

I later asked Lonnie Frey and Frank McCormick about my odd conversation with Myers. I learned that the previous year Billy had dropped a couple of routine pop-ups. The Cincinnati sportswriters had criticized him, and the fans had become so negative that his confidence plummeted. As a result, Myers, as good a defensive shortstop as there was in the league, was shying away from infield pop-ups.

The Reds had finished fourth in 1938, six games behind the pennant-winning Cubs, and a dramatic improvement over their cellar-dwelling performance in 1937. We believed we had a real shot at the pennant in

1939, so I took it upon myself to seek out the writers covering the team. I asked them to write more favorably about Myers and, if he miscued, to write about someone else. The writers came through for us. On opening day at Crosley Field against the Pittsburgh Pirates, a full house gave Myers a resounding round of applause on his first at-bat. That got Billy on the way to what would become his finest year in the big leagues. He fielded exceptionally well and hit .281, up 28 percentage points over 1938. The Reds won their first pennant in twenty years and Billy played an integral role in our success, thanks to the support of the Cincinnati fans.

Baseball fans really can affect the outcome of ballgames and can even impact how a team finishes in the standings. Their support or lack of it can be instrumental in a team's success or failure. It is difficult to ignore them when things go wrong, although I did my best not to let them affect me either way while I played. In my own time, I experienced both extreme kindnesses and, on occasion, uncouth behavior from fans. I learned early in my career that a ballplayer has to learn to take the good with the bad.

Baseball endures, however, because of its wonderful, caring and rabid fans. Even today, fifty-seven years after my last major league ballgame, I get several letters a week from fans asking for my autograph and, as often as not, about some aspect of my playing days. For better or worse, baseball is and always has been for the fans.

9 THE UMPIRES

By and large, an adversorial relationship exists between umpires and ballplayers. Even so, they get along rather well—at least they did in the 1930s when I played. And the umpires then had responsibility for making more decisions than umpires do today, for there were only two of them on the field, one behind the plate and one covering the bases.

The ballplayers of the '30s were competitive and skilled. After all, there were only twenty-four players on a team and only sixteen clubs in the big leagues. For the most part, the players were young, with good eyesight and exceptional reflexes. They were hardly objective, however, and were inclined to favor themselves on all close calls. The umpires were older, experienced, impartial, and not concerned with who won or lost, or who might get their feelings hurt in the process. They made a conscientious effort to call them as they saw them. The umpires were and are an integral part of the game, a fact that was driven home to me with that first at-bat of mine in the big leagues.

Although umpires are supposed to control the game and their own tempers, they are human. Lou Kolls was normally a very pleasant guy, willing to discuss the happenings of the day. Before that full house at League Park in Cleveland one day, however, he lost his cool with the Ferrell brothers, and they spectacularly lost theirs with him. Lou got so mad he invited Rick and Wes to meet him under the stands after the game with a promise to lick them both. As far as I know, there was no rumble under the stands after the game.

Harry Geisel was the most formal and dignified of the umpires of the 1930s, tall, straight-backed, and meticulous in his dress. Once when I was with the Athletics, we were in Detroit to play the Tigers on a Sunday afternoon. Briggs Stadium was filled nearly to capacity in spite of a steady drizzle. The field was in poor shape from the rain, with pools of water in the outfield and a thin, slick layer of mud in the infield. The Detroit ownership, of course, wanted to start the game and hoped to get in 5-1/2 innings so it could reap the profits from the large crowd. Geisel was the home-plate umpire and controlled the game once it began. He thought it should have been postponed. He had no interest in spending the afternoon in the rain, but when I came up to leadoff, he said, "It's idiocy, but we're going to play the whole nine innings."

He was wrong. In the bottom of the fifth, a Detroit batter lifted a high pop foul toward the A's dugout and Frank Hayes, our catcher, ran after it. Geisel, on top of the play, ran over behind Frank. Hayes stopped and planted

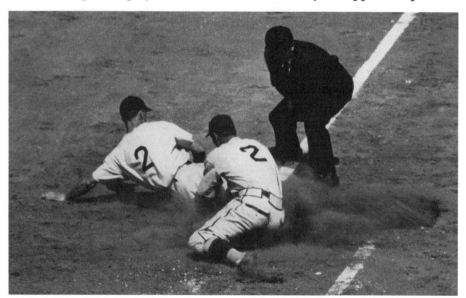

Just back to the bag. The author avoids a pickoff attempt while with the Red Sox. The first baseman is Jack Burns of the St. Louis Browns and the umpire poised to make the call is John Quinn.

under the ball. Behind him, Geisel tried to stop as well, but his feet flew out from under him and he landed on his back in the in the middle of the mud in front of the dugout. Thoroughly soaked and with his dignity ruffled, he got up and said, "That's it. The game is called. Everybody go home." We did.

George Moriarty had played third base for thirteen years in the big leagues, seven of them with Ty Cobb and the Tigers. He later managed Detroit for two years before turning to umpiring. Legend had it that he had fought and whipped Cobb during his playing days. Maybe so, maybe not. I never took the trouble to find out, but he was a pretty good umpire.

George sometimes had trouble leaving his playing and managing days behind. He had a habit of coaching base runners, especially those capable of playing the speed game of his youth. For example, if I was on first in a steal situation, Morarity would actually get into the game and coach me. "Take a little more lead," he would advise. "You can take more lead than that. I'm not gonna call you out." George loved to get to the ballpark early, put on his blue uniform and chew the fat in the dugout during batting practice. He reminded me there that when the conditions were right, a fast runner could sometimes steal second on a base on balls, as I later did three times. Old George loved baseball and never could get enough of it.

Bill McGowan umpired in the American League for twenty-nine years. He was arrogant, chesty, and sufficient unto himself. He claimed he had never missed a call and, to tell the truth, he was the best of the lot. He hustled and he concentrated hard whether he was behind the plate or working the bases. He was not well-liked, but he was well-respected.

McGowan was behind the plate on the famous occasion when in the late afternoon shadows Lefty Gomez carried a flaming cigarette lighter to the plate against Bob Feller. McGowan's reaction to Lefty's prank was to tell him, "Put out that lighter. You're making a farce of the game." Asked later if he had trouble seeing Feller on the mound, Lefty said, "I could see him all right, I just wanted to make sure he could see me."

Bill had a bad off-season habit: he loved to play the horses. One winter he called me at my house in College Park, Maryland, from his home in Washington, D.C. He said he had experienced some financial misfortune and asked if I could lend him a few hundred dollars to tide him over a month or two. I sent him a check for the amount requested, but he failed to repay me on time. Now umpires get paid for spring training games although players do not, so during the spring I dropped Bill a note reminding him of his overdue obligation. He did not reply. I wrote again and suggested that if I did not hear from him I would bring the matter to the attention of Commissioner Landis. His check came by the next mail and it was good. To give the guy his due, I can recall no ill will or any questionable decisions against me. As I said, he worked hard and took his responsibilities seriously.

Bill Klem was just as efficient, respected, and arrogant in the National League. He could be a truculent old buzzard, but he was an excellent umpire. He let it be known through his business-like demeanor and his quick thumb over any perceived effrontery that he was in control of the game. He had a face like a pug and I had always heard ballplayers refer to Klem as "Catfish." I somehow missed learning that he loathed the name. He was behind the plate on our first trip to Forbes Field in Pittsburgh after I came over to the National League in 1939. I was the leadoff batter for the Reds in the first inning and, wanting to ingratiate myself with the famed arbiter, I gave him my very best smile and said, "Good afternoon, Catfish." Off came his mask, the tobacco juice flew, and he said to me in no uncertain terms, "Young man, you're new in this league. Don't you ever call me Catfish again." And I didn't.

George Magerkurth, he who was attacked at Ebbets Field, was another noteworthy National League umpire, a big fellow with a head like a pumpkin and a jaw swollen with an ever-present chaw of tobacco. Although he got himself into a lot of scraps, players liked him. In one game, Reds center fielder Harry Craft hit a towering fly into the left field stands in the

Billy Jurges, one fiery competitor.

Polo Grounds in a close game against the Giants. It was clear to everyone on both teams that the ball carried to the left of the foul pole, but Magerkurth, behind the plate, saw it differently. He ruled the ball fair and Craft had a home run.

The inaccuracy of the call infuriated the Giants' captain, Billy Jurges, and he raced in from shortstop to lodge a vehement complaint. Bill got his nose too close to Magerkurth's, and as a result was the unhappy recipient of sprayed tobacco juice when George replied with some heat. Jurges thought George was spitting at him, so he let fly a full load of spit in return, all to the lusty cheers of the Reds dugout. Since the call had gone our way, we thought the entire episode was a riot. Needless to say, Jurges was through for the afternoon.

For the most part, of course, umpires had the upper hand and effectively controlled the game. They would take a lot of grief from the players or managers, and only when extremely rough language was used or physical contact was made would they eject someone. Some umpires, like Babe Pinelli and Beans Reardon, enjoyed socializing with the players, and before games would drop into the dugouts to visit. It must have helped, because these umpires seemed to have relatively little trouble during the games. Other umpires avoided this kind of familiarity.

I had my ups and downs with umpires, especially with Larry Goetz, a fine National Leaguer whom I respected greatly. Larry was lean and hard, and able to call a good game during the dog days of August when the temperature hit a hundred and the doubleheaders piled up. He enjoyed a little conversation when you came up to the plate and would often begin it. Accordingly, he and I had a bit of a colloquy one evening in Cincinnati during one of our seven permissible night games in 1940. It was late in the season, and Max Butcher of the Pirates was pitching against us. Butcher always seemed to pitch well against the Reds and this game was no exception. We were in the bottom of the thirteenth when the first Reds batter walked and was sacrificed to second, making it my turn to bat. As I approached the plate, Larry removed his mask and in an exhausted, almost pleading voice, said, "Bill, let's get this thing over with. I'm tired." "Larry," I responded, "I'm the best man in the league in a situation like this." With that I smacked Butcher's first pitch on a line between center and right to drive in the winning run. Sometimes it is better to be lucky than good. Since we were headed to our second pennant that summer there was a capacity crowd in the stands, as there was for all of our night games. When I got that hit I was told their roar could be heard in downtown Cincinnati. I remember the event because Larry Goetz related it verbatim to Warren Giles, the Reds general manager, and Mr. Giles told the story twenty years later at the Netherlands Plaza Hotel at a luncheon honoring the World Champions of 1940.

In 1942, again late in the summer, I was playing third base for the New

York Giants and came to bat in the Polo Grounds. Goetz was the umpire behind the plate. Again, as I approach the batter's box, he took off his mask and in a sad voice said, "Of all the guys in the league, I never expected you would do this to us."

I immediately knew that Larry was referring to that article in *The Saturday Evening Post* that Harold Parrott had turned into an unbalanced blast at the fans. There were a few negative things in there about umpires, too. Goetz was hurt by it and let me know. I didn't blame him. Even now, over a half-century later, I wish I'd had the chance to object to the title, and rewrite that article so that it said what I really meant.

10 THE ENIGMA

Intellectual attainment during my days in the big leagues, 1930-1942, was strictly frowned upon. If you unwittingly used a phrase like "magna cum laude," your listener, if you had one, would disappear. As a matter of fact, brains were indicative of mediocre baseball performance. Productiveness per time at bat was thought to bear an inverse relationship to one's I.Q. I played with nine of the ten most productive hitters of all time per time at bat. They were not distinguished by their scholarly backgrounds. Only one of them, Lou Gehrig, who had a couple of years at Columbia, had attended college.

Moe Berg was cut from a different piece of cloth. He was a magna cum laude graduate of Princeton where he also starred at shortstop for the varsity baseball team. He majored in modern languages and studied no fewer than seven: Latin, Greek, French, Spanish, Italian, German, and Sanskrit. The Brooklyn Dodgers signed him at the age of twenty-one and he appeared in 49 games for the Dodgers in 1923, mostly at shortstop. He hit only .186, however, and spent the next three years in the minors before the Chicago White Sox plucked him from Reading after the 1925 season. There he hit an impressive .311 and batted in 124 runs. Still a shortstop, however, he had committed 72 sobering errors.

He appeared in 41 games for the 1926 White Sox, 31 at shortstop, but hit just .221. His development was no doubt hindered by his off-season activities. He studied French and Spanish at Columbia's Graduate School of Arts and Sciences and then began law school, also at Columbia. As a result, early in his career Moe did not have the benefit of spring training, usually reporting for baseball duty in late May or early June.

In 1927, Berg became a catcher by pure happenstance. Chicago's regular catchers were Harry McCurdy and Buck Crouse. Ray Schalk was the manager and, at thirty-five, he still liked to catch now and again when he felt up to it. He got hurt in late July when Julie Wera of the Yankees ran over him at the plate. A few days later, Crouse split a finger in Philadelphia. On to Boston went the Pale Hose with only one catcher left and he did not last long. Red Sox outfielder Cleo Carlyle bowled McCurdy over in the third inning and knocked him out of action. Schalk, stunned by this turn of events, registered his dismay in the dugout. In a low voice, Berg said, "You've got a big league catcher right here." As the story goes, Berg was referring to first baseman Earl Sheely, who had caught some in the minor leagues. But Schalk misunderstood. "All right, Berg. Get in there," he said. Moe dutifully began buckling on the so-called "tools of ignorance" for the first time since his boyhood days on the Newark sandlots. He is reputed to have said, "If the worst happens, kindly deliver the body to Newark."

The move was most fortuitous for Moe. From 1927 until his retirement from baseball in 1939, he was solely a catcher. With his weak bat and slowness afoot, it is doubtful that he would have had a very long major league career as a shortstop. As a backup catcher, those shortcomings were less important. He ended up playing fifteen years, appearing in but 662 games with a .243 lifetime average. By far his best year was 1929, when he was the White Sox's regular catcher, batting a solid .288 in 106 games.

In spite of that fine year, Moe was destined to spend the majority of his career in the bullpen, answering the phone and warming up pitchers. Mostly what he did in the bullpen, though, was sit and watch, with lots of time for discourse. There he'd be, commenting on the game with the country boys who had strong arms and strong backs, chewed Brown Mule, and swore like sailors. But Moe must have felt at home. He stayed in the bullpen for twelve years.

Moe became my teammate in Boston in 1935, after Tom Yawkey purchased Joe Cronin from Washington to manage the Red Sox. Joe brought Berg and Al Schacht with him, Schacht as a coach. The two of them couldn't have been more different. For starters, Al probably never finished high school. He would pitch batting practice and coach third base each day. Moe pontificated in the dugout until it was time to go do the same in the bullpen. Al was full of fun, always laughing and kidding. Moe was sober, almost sorrowful, always carrying the *Wall Street Journal* under his arm.

Coaching third, Al was close to the visitors' dugout at Fenway. When his former Washington teammates came to town, he was the target of a considerable amount of bench jockeying. On one occasion, Ed Linke, a burly pitcher, was on Al pretty brutally and challenged him to fight. Al weighed maybe 140 dripping wet, about forty pounds less than Linke, who was also twenty years his junior. Nevertheless, Al waited for him in the Red Sox dugout and offered his body for the mauling. Instead of swinging a fist, Linke used his superior strength to throw Schacht to the dugout floor and attempted to punch him in the face while he was down. Several Red Sox pulled Linke off and sent him on his way. We left Boston by train that evening for a trip west, and Al was sitting beside Moe on a Pullman seat. I was proud of Al's courage, so I approached him, stuck out my hand and said, "Al, you showed me something today. You were willing to fight when you knew you had no chance." Berg looked at me with contempt and snarled, "Dogs fight."

By now it should be obvious that Moe and I did not see eye to eye. I always felt that he had the tools to have caught every day. He was six-foot-one, weighed a solid 185 pounds, moved well, had a good arm, knew the hitters, and with a little determination could have been a good hitter. His habits were exemplary. He did not smoke, chew, drink, or carouse.

Although he did not show it often, Moe had a sense of humor. My old friend Shirley Povich, the legendary sportswriter for the Washington *Post*, tells of a time with the Senators when Moe roomed with Dave Harris, a

Moe Berg: A lot of brains and some brawn.

good-hitting outfielder. Harris thought Moe knew everything except how to hit. Known as Sheriff—because he looked like one, not because he was one—Harris was from rural North Carolina and had little formal education. According to Povich, one morning during spring training in Biloxi, Mississippi, Harris missed his customary breakfast with Berg. Moe later found him in the hotel lobby in street clothes when the rest of the team was in uniform to ride to the ballpark. Moe asked the Sheriff if anything was wrong.

"Believe it or not, I'm not feeling well," said Harris. "First sick day I ever had in my life. Don't know what is wrong but my stomach's jumping. The skipper [manager Walter Johnson] told me to take the day off."

Berg looked the Sheriff over intently. "Let me see your tongue," he said knowingly. Obediently Harris stuck out his tongue. Moe peered at it closely. "You'll be all right," he said with a quick nod to the nearby Povich. "Just lay off the heavy food and get some rest today. In the morning you'll be your old self. You've just got a slight case of intestinal fortitude." The next morning the Sheriff bounced down to breakfast. "Feel great, Moe," he said. "You were right. That little touch of intestinal fortitude I had is all gone."

Moe liked the life of a ballplayer, the good pay, the short hours, the prestige. But he had little stomach for the heat of battle or the sweat from catching in hundred-degree heat. Catching daily is the hardest, hottest, dirtiest job on the team. The equipment is heavy and the punishment is constant. Moe's attitude was "to hell with it. I'll sit in the shade in the bullpen and ruminate." And he did, for many, many years.

The contrast with Rick Ferrell, our regular catcher, was striking. Rick weighed about 150 pounds and caught 131 games in 1935. He frequently caught second games of doubleheaders in the heat of the summer. Berg did not seem to mind, sometimes advising manager Cronin to leave Ferrell in there because he was doing such a good job. We all thought Moe was lazy. He seemed to prefer talking baseball to playing it. Off the field, Berg kept his own counsel. He made it pretty clear he did not want to join the boys for a movie or for dinner, so we never asked him.

We were teammates during the 1935 and 1936 seasons, after which I was traded to the Athletics. I ran into him in Washington during the war, in 1943 or 1944, when we were both out of baseball. It was on Pennsylvania Avenue in front of the White House. Moe was walking briskly west, neatly groomed, his trademark *Wall Street Journal* under his left arm. We greeted as old friends and associates should and I said, "What brings you to Washington, Moe?"

"Oh, a bit of this and that," he volunteered. Moe was always on the secretive side, but I did get from him that he was with the State Department. I had no reason to disbelieve him, since he was walking in the direction of the old State, War and Navy Building. It was only a good many years later, after his death in 1972, that I read that he was a spy and that it was from Moe's photographs of Tokyo taken during a 1934 postseason All-Star barnstorming trip to Japan that Jimmy Doolittle directed his bombing raids. Nicholas Davidoff, in his bestselling biography, *The Catcher Was A Spy: The Mysterious Life of Moe Berg*, debunks that theory, although Berg did make his 1934 photos, taken mainly from the top of St. Luke's Hospital in Tokyo, available to military intelligence. According to Davidoff, U.S. military intelligence had by then much more detailed information about Tokyo.

It is clear that Berg worked first for the Office of Inter-American Affairs and then the Office of Strategic Services, the precursor to the CIA, during World War II, and was heavily involved in U.S. intelligence. He was even involved in a proposed plot to kidnap Werner Heisenberg, one of the leading German atomic physicists.

According to his biographer, Moe's eccentricities finally got the best of him and the last years of his life were spent as a reclusive loner, without funds and relying on an ever-dwindling assortment of friends and family for financial support. Al Schacht for years had a restaurant in midtown Manhattan that was popular among ballplayers and ex-ballplayers. Moe owed both Al and Toots Shor for meals and drinks. Moe Berg was a brilliant man and a decent baseball player who could have been a much better one. I think his life was very sad.

11 THE VALUE OF HUSTLE

Power is king! There was always a thrill in seeing Babe Ruth catch hold of one and send it flying over the right field wall. Even in the days of Ruth, Foxx, and Gehrig, however, the mightiest slugger would come up off the end of the bat with two strikes in the interest of just meeting the ball. If you stayed down on the end of the bat and continued to flail away instead of making contact, you would hear about it from your team-mates—and your manager.

I am not certain when the change in attitude occurred, but I do remember a conversation with George Selkirk one sunny afternoon on the golf course at Columbia Country Club. It was the early 1960s, and George was the general manager of the Washington Senators. He had been a fine, hard-hitting outfielder with the Yankees from 1934 through 1942 and played on pennant winners in '36, '37, '38, '39, '41, and '42. Those were smart, hard-nosed Yankee ball clubs with a tough manager, Joe McCarthy, and they won by team effort.

The subject of our conversation was Frank Howard, a big moose of a man playing left field for the Senators. Frank was a former basketball play-er at Ohio State who stood six-foot-seven and weighed in at about 255. I had watched him play a time or two when he took full cuts and struck out with men in scoring position. "George," I asked my guest, "why don't you speak to Howard and get him to shorten his swing when runners are on second or third?"

Selkirk moaned, "Bill, I've spoken to him a hundred times about shortening up with two strikes and just putting wood on the ball. The attitude today is that home run hitters drive Cadillacs and singles hitters drive Fords."

The Senators were at the time in last place in the American League.

When I came up with the Yankees, it quickly became apparent that the leaders of that great ballclub would not brook a lack of effort. Ruth, Gehrig, and Bill Dickey played hard and wanted to win, and if you did anything to interfere with winning they would get on you hard—and if they got on you, you'd better take what was coming and keep your mouth shut.

Bill Dickey was the heart of the team defensively and commanded tremendous respect from the Yankee pitchers. Once the game started, he ran the show. He was smart. He studied the opposing hitters' strengths and weaknesses and calling the game accordingly. If Lefty Gomez or Red Ruffing or any other pitcher seemed to be losing his concentration, Dickey would walk a third of the way to the mound and fire the ball back at them to get their attention.

The Yankees disciplined each other. For example, no one ever ate on the bench, despite what some of the movies have shown. Ruth and others just would not have tolerated it. Mostly, they led by example. I remember an occasion when an opposing batter hit a shot between Gehrig and first base down into the right field corner. Ruth fielded the ball deep in right and threw to cutoff man Tony Lazzeri, who threw wildly to Joe Sewell at third base. The runner was in at third, but he couldn't score on the bad throw, because Gehrig had raced across the infield to back up the play. When you saw that kind of hustle, you knew you had to go all-out yourself to be accepted by Gehrig, and every young Yankee wanted that acceptance.

In my era, I learned early that alertness, awareness, quick thinking, and simple hustle were highly prized by big league ballplayers. Early in my career my friend Ben Chapman taught me about resourcefulness and aggressive play when I was playing third base for the Boston Red Sox against his Yankees at the Stadium. He was stretching his luck, trying to go from first to third on a single to right field. Roy Johnson had a strong arm and his throw had Chapman beat by five or six feet. I made a mistake, though. I laid my glove with the ball in it right in his path, figuring he'd slide into it and tag himself out. Instead, Ben slid on his right hip and scissor-kicked my wrist with his left foot, sending the ball flying. He then hollered at the umpire, "He's holding me, he's holding me." Indeed I was. He was not going anywhere until someone retrieved the ball.

On defense and on the bases, I learned to concentrate hard and to try and think a step or two ahead of the game. This often paid off. For example, once when I was playing third base for the Athletics against the Senators in Griffith Stadium, Buddy Lewis, a smart, fast runner, was on second with two out in a close ball game. John Stone, a good lefthanded batter, hitting around .340, and a fast runner to boot, was at the plate. He was a pull hitter, so the infield shifted left in anticipation. Against the odds, however, Stone hit a slow, high chopper in fair territory just inside the third base line. I ran toward the bounding ball, fielded it backhanded, took it from my glove with my right hand and prepared to throw to first as hard as I could to try to nip Stone. As I was doing all this, I saw Lewis running hard toward third. Since he was a good, aggressive baserunner, I knew he would round third to be in position to score if I made a bad throw. I also knew that my chances of getting Stone at first were slim. So my hard throw to first was without the ball, which was still in my hand. I turned and took off after Lewis who was well down the line toward home. Clyde Milan, the Washington third-base coach, was screaming, "Get back! Get back!" I can see Buddy Lewis's eyes to this day. He looked like a startled doe. He scrambled and dove for the bag and I dove and tagged him out. The inning was over and Stone was robbed of an infield hit.

On the base paths, I liked to take calculated risks just like Buddy Lewis. In August, 1934, the league-leading Detroit Tigers were in Fenway Park to play my Red Sox. Schoolboy Rowe had won fifteen straight ballgames and was hoping to make it sixteen against us. We were in third place, still in the pennant race, and some 35,000 noisy fans filled the park.

It was before this game that umpire George Moriarty made the suggestion of stealing second on a base on balls, which I've already mentioned. I told him I'd never tried it. Old-timer George was so fond of good baserunning that he told me how it could be done. In the sixth or seventh inning the Tigers were one run ahead. Rowe was a bit on the wild side, and I coaxed a walk to lead off the inning. Jogging to first, I looked at Bill Rogell at shortstop and Charlie Gehringer at second. Both had their backs to the infield, tapping clods of earth with their spikes. About fifteen feet before first, I put it into high gear and touched the base under a full head of steam. The crowd roar could probably be heard all the way to the Back Bay station. Ray Hayworth, the Tiger catcher, still had the ball in his hand and threw to second, which was covered by no one. The ball bounded out to JoJo White in center field while I slid into second, bounced up, and scurried to third. From there I soon scored the tying run. I would like to report that this bit of histrionics won the ballgame, but it did not. Rowe hung in there and won his sixteenth straight in the thirteenth inning.

Alertness and hustle did help win the opening game of the 1935 season. The Red Sox were in Yankee Stadium on a sunny but windy day and 60,000 people were in the stands. Wes Ferrell, who had suffered through a miserable spring training, hooked up against Yankee ace Lefty Gomez. Wesley had a shaky start, walking the first two men before he attacked the mound with his spikes to make it more suitable, creating a dust storm in the process. He got out of the inning unscathed and a classic pitching duel ensued. By the top of the ninth the game was still scoreless.

I led off, reached base, and got to third with one out. Outfielder Carl Reynolds struck out on a pitch that bounced out of Bill Dickey's glove. Carl took off for first base. Dickey quickly scrambled after the ball, which was a bit in front and to the side of the plate, and fired to Gehrig to retire Reynolds. I edged off third, and as soon as Dickey's arm dropped, I took off for home. Gehrig's hasty return throw was a little high, and I was able to slide safely across the plate with the game's only run. Wesley retired the Yankees in the bottom of the ninth to preserve our 1-0 victory.

Lefty Gomez did anything he could to gain an edge, even off the field. Lefty was a charmer who, I became convinced, used his good nature to seek a competitive advantage. It seemed to me that he liked to hang around the opposing team's clubhouse or bench a little too much before games, joking and carrying on, particularly on the day before he was to pitch. He was even quoted as saying, "I talk 'em out of hits." One day in Yankee Stadium when I was with the Red Sox, I had my game face on when Lefty came sauntering into our clubhouse. After a few minutes, I finally had enough of his distraction and popped him across his left arm and told him to get the hell out of our clubhouse. He glanced at me with a hurt look and left. I wanted to beat him, not laugh at his jokes.

I was fortunate enough to lead the American League in stolen bases in 1934, 1935, and 1937. Base stealers have to be fast, and I could run in those years. Slow runners, obviously, are not base stealers. Ernie Lombardi caught for seventeen years in the big leagues and is credited with eight stolen bases in 1,853 games. I've never been amazed that he had so few. In fact, I've always wondered how Ernie got that many. Ernie was S-L-O-W.

For me at least, training for base stealing began at an early age. When I was five or six years old, my mother would send me on errands around our neighborhood and I would run to and from my destination as fast as I could. I loved to run, and I kept on running through grade school, high school, and college. Almost before I knew it, I was the fastest man on the New York Yankees (although Chapman could push me to the limit in any race). All that running I did as a kid really did pay off in baseball.

Of course, many ballplayers are fast, but not that many are good base stealers. Good judgment, instinct, and a willingness to learn the pitcher's *normal* pitching patterns are all important factors. I italicized "normal" because crafty pitchers vary their cadence to confuse the base runner.

In the '30s, game situations controlled whether a stolen base was in order. If you were eight or nine runs ahead, there was no advantage to stealing, risking injury, and provoking the opposition. The same was true if you were a bunch of runs down. The single run you represented was insignificant; you needed a cluster.

The makeup of the team and the manager's approach to the game also dictated how much stealing was encouraged. For example, with the 1931 Yankees, Ben Chapman stole 61 bases to lead the American League by a wide margin. He probably could have stolen 100, but with Ruth, Gehrig, Lazzeri, and Dickey behind him, it would have been foolhardy to take chances on the basepaths. Manager Joe McCarthy knew Ben had the speed to score from first on any balls hit into the gaps. The same was true for me when I played for pennant-winning teams in Cincinnati. Bill McKechnie discouraged me from taking risks on the basepaths because hitting behind me were Frank McCormick, Ernie Lombardi, and Ival Goodman, all long-ball and high percentage hitters with men on base. As a result I stole only fifteen and sixteen bases in our two pennant years.

In Cincinnati, we won baseball games by good pitching and defensive play as much as by offense. The world champion Reds of 1940 played their 77 home games in an average of one hour and forty minutes. I think we accomplished this largely because we had exceptional defense and pitchers with good control who got hitters to hit the ball to us early in the count.

Not surprisingly, a great, hustling defensive play was the key to our first pennant in 1939. It happened in an important late season series with the St. Louis Cardinals, who were right on our tail. Ival Goodman, heads up all the way, raced over from right field to corral the carom of a ball Joe Medwick had clubbed over Harry Craft's head in center. He pounced on the ball like a big cat, whirled, and threw the surprised Medwick out at third by twenty feet. I know because I caught the ball. The play broke the Cardinals' back and opened the door for our pennant. That was the kind of play that won us games and that made me so proud to be a member of the Reds of that era.

12 THE DIZ, BOBO, KING CARL AND THE WANER BOYS

My era produced not only some of the great ballplayers of all time but also some of the greatest characters the game has known. Dizzy Dean certainly fits in both categories. Diz was, of course, the leader of the famous St. Louis Cardinals Gashouse Gang of the 1930's, leading the team to the 1934 world championship and generally livening up baseball for a decade. Before he hurt his arm, he was an overpowering flamethrower, winning 30 games in 1934, 28 in 1935, and 24 in 1936. He was a country boy who loved to have a good time and was not shy about making predictions. During spring training in 1934, he boldly predicted that "Me'n Paul will win 45 games." Paul was his brother, dubbed Daffy by the sportswriters although he was pretty quiet—at least compared to Dizzy. What made the prediction laughable was that Paul had never before pitched in the big leagues. Dizzy was coming off of his first 20-win season, along with 18 losses. As the world now knows, the Dean brothers proceeded to win 49 games as the Cardinals took the the pennant and the World Series. Paul won 19 in his rookie year to complement Dizzy's 30. During the pennant drive in September, Dizzy shut out the Brooklyn Dodgers on three hits in the first game of a doubleheader. Paul pitched a no-hitter in the nightcap, famously prompting Dizzy to say, "I wished I'da knowed Paul was goin' to pitch a no-hitter. I'da pitched one, too."

He probably would have. He had a crackling curve ball to go with a smoking fastball, and the savvy born of a hard life. Although he was famous for his colorful butchering of the English language and his malapropisms ("the runners returned to their respectable bases"), Dizzy was sharp. Jimmie Wilson told me about a day in St. Louis when he was managing the Phillies. They were having their pregame meeting to discuss how to pitch to the Cardinal lineup when Dizzy Dean walked in. That in itself was unheard-of, but Dean was Dean. "Gimmie that lineup card," he said. "I'll tell you how to pitch to those sonuvabitches." He took the card and went down the entire Cardinal lineup, telling the Phillies how to pitch to the likes of Ducky Medwick, Johnny Mize, and Walker Cooper. Wilson told me, "You know, the bugger got it exactly right on every hitter. He told us how to pitch to his own teammates."

St. Louis could be miserably hot and humid in the summer. One day Dizzy and teammate Pepper Martin decided it was too hot to play the second game of a doubleheader, so they dragged an old blanket out of the dugout and built a fire on the field with some paper and kindling. They somehow had a couple of peace pipes and sat by the fire and started smoking them, with the blanket wrapped around them.

On another occasion, an off-day for the Cardinals in Philadephia, Martin and Dean got hold of some overalls and striped caps. They put them on and disrupted a meeting at the hotel by going in and moving tables and taking some pictures off the wall. Then they pretended to get into an argument about what was to be moved next and Dizzy hauled off and "slugged" Pepper, hitting Martin's hand next to his face and scoring an apparent clean knockout. Someone in the group finally recognized them as Cardinals and asked them to talk about baseball. Eventually, Dizzy spied someone at the head table they had not noticed before: their manager, Frankie Frisch. According to Dizzy, "Frisch had just two words for us: 'I am mortified.'"

Bobo Newsom was called Bobo because he called everybody else Bobo. Sort of makes sense, I guess. He was also frequently called Buck, though I'm not sure why. I do know that he pitched in the big leagues in four different decades, beginning in 1929 when he was twenty-one and not ending until

Country-smart fireballer Dizzy Dean.

1953 when he was past his forty-sixth birthday. His lifetime record was a sub-.500 211 wins and 222 losses, but he was a three-time 20-game winner and pitched in two World Series. His peak was with the 1940 Detroit Tigers. There, as the ace of the staff, he won 21 games and lost only five, despite missing three weeks with a broken thumb. In doing so, he led the Tigers to the pennant by a scant game over the Cleveland Indians, with the vaunted Yankees a game further back.

I never liked Bobo Newsom, probably because he represented the antithesis of all that I thought myself to be. Whenever he was on the mound with the Browns, Senators, or Tigers during my playing days, I was on him and I made no bones about the fact that he was not my favorite person. Once when he pitched for the Senators and I came to town with the Red Sox for a series, he hired our clubhouse boy Freddie Baxter to hang a large sign that covered the entire front of my locker. It read "How are you today, my friend? Bobo." My teammates and I enjoyed that immensely, but it did not alter my normal routine of riding Newsom.

Bobo was a good pitcher with a rubber arm and a head to match, as was demonstrated one hot afternoon in Griffith Stadium. Bobo was pitching against my Red Sox when Senators' third baseman Ossie Bluege, charging in to field a topped roller, fired a hard submarine throw to Joe Kuhel at first. Bobo managed to get in the line of fire and Bluege's throw hit him squarely in the head. Old Bobo was laid out on the grass like a piece of carpet, and there he stayed until revived with a bucket of ice water. Any ordinary ballplayer would have been carted off on a stretcher to an ambulance, but not Bobo. He picked up his glove, put his hat back on his head, and pitched the rest of the ballgame. Whether he won or lost I do not remember, but in retrospect I sort of hope he won.

Newsom came from the hinterlands of South Carolina, back in the bush, miles from any main highway. He did not have the benefit of much schooling and even indoor plumbing was a stranger to him. In fact, his backhouse was the place in which one of his down-home buddies pulled a prank that almost did old Bobo in. Bobo's backhouse was a wooden two-holer that happened to back up to a pig pen. Its door was fastened by a knob with a nail driven through it and a Sears catalogue handy. There one morning after breakfast Bobo sat, meditated, and listened to the pigs grunt. His "friend" quietly vaulted over the pigpen fence, made his way to the backhouse and, reaching up and over a protective board while grunting like an old boar, grabbed ahold of Bobo's private parts. There followed a terrified bellow from within the privy, and Bobo exited, door and all.

Another story I heard about Bobo involved Jim Berryman, political cartoonist for the Washington *Star*, as his daddy had been before him, and Francis Stann-Berryman, a featured sportswriter with the same paper. Francis had been in the same class at Central High School with my younger sister. He had become an excellent writer who did a superb job whether on baseball, football, or horse racing. He wielded a gentle pen, never sharp. In mid-February one year, these two colleagues were on their way south by automobile to cover the Senators in spring training. Near Florence, South Carolina, Francis suggested they take a detour and drop by to see Newsom, who was holding out at home for a better contract from Clark Griffith. Stann-Berryman described their visit to me as follows:

"We found the Newsom house back on a country road. It wasn't much of a place. The steps leading up to the front porch were in disrepair, as was the porch itself. The screen door had a good size hole punched in it through which several small sized rabbit dogs freely accessed. Bobo was at home, happy to see us and ushered us into his living room where Mrs. Newsom sat on a sofa, breast feeding a baby. The talk soon got to baseball, his holdout, spring training in Orlando, Florida, the hotel, and finally the babe in the cocktail lounge at the hotel. Bobo allowed as to how he would take a crack at that if she was still there. Mrs. Newsom heard but made no comment. We had a good visit and went on our way south."

Bobo's personal habits notwithstanding, the guy could pitch. He was a workhorse who wanted the ball and he knew what he was doing. He was

Bobo Newsom and Paul Derringer before Game One of the
1940 World Series. The rascals sure could pitch.

shrewd, sanguine, and businesslike on the mound, and a great deal smarter than the impression you got from him off the field. The 1940 World Series was a good example of Bobo's savvy, toughness, and durability. Detroit manager Del Baker selected him to start the opening game against us in Cincinnati against Paul Derringer. The Tigers struck for five runs in the second and Bobo coasted to a 7-2 victory. But triumph soon turned to tragedy. Bobo's father, Henry Louis Newsom, and other members of the family had traveled to Cincinnati to see Buck in his first World Series. The game and the celebration were too much for the elder Newsom, who died of a heart attack at his hotel the night after the game.

Nonetheless, Newsom, one tough competitor, came back to pitch Game 5 in Detroit, with the Series tied 2-2. In a game he dedicated to his father, Bobo held us to three singles to beat us, 8-0. The Series moved back

to Cincinnati the next day for Game 6. The Reds prevailed, 4-0, behind
Bucky Walters' five-hit shutout, setting up Game 7 to decide the World
Championship. To no one's surprise, Baker sent Bobo to the mound with
only one day's rest to face Derringer again. Bobo took a 1-0 lead into the
bottom of the seventh when we struck for the two runs that won the Series.
Although defeated, Newsom's Series performance was remarkable. In his
three starts he pitched 26 innings, striking out 17, while walking only four.
He allowed 18 hits and four runs for a minuscule 1.38 earned run average.
We were most fortunate to beat him in Game 7.

A week or so later, I joined an all-star team that Rick and Wes Ferrell
assembled to play exhibition games in Durham and Salisbury, North
Carolina. Herb Pennock, the former Yankee pitching great, was along to
help run the trip. After the game in Durham, I accompanied Herb to the
Duke University campus to visit Bob Carpenter, the boy I'd been assigned
to take to the movies when I'd been a Yankee rookie, who was by then a
student at Duke. It was fairly late when we returned to our hotel, only to
find the irrepressible Bobo Newsom fast asleep in Pennock's bed, with
mouth open catching flies. He had not been invited by the Ferrells to get
in on the action, but had read about it in a newspaper and driven up from
South Carolina for a visit. How he got into Herb's room, I still do not know.
Bobo Newsom—one of a kind.

Except for his prowess on the mound, Carl Hubbell could not have
been more different than Dizzy Dean or Bobo Newsom. Carl was quiet,
introspective, and a model of decorum. He did not have an aggressive bone
in his body, and he had a sly sense of humor that made him enjoyable to
be around. In spite of his different temperament, or perhaps because of it,
Hubbell was Diz's equal on the mound. By the time we became teammates
with the 1942 Giants, we were both near the end of the line. Carl was battling arm trouble from years of throwing his famed screwball (his left hand
and arm were permanently turned outward). He still managed an 11-8
record with 11 complete games in 20 starts.

Still, he was only a shadow of what he had been, one of the greatest lefthanders of all time. From the Oklahoma oilfields, he put together five consecutive 20-win seasons, beginning in 1933, and pitched the Giants to pennants in 1933, 1936, and 1937. In 1933, his first of two Most Valuable Player award seasons, he won 23 games, threw ten shutouts, and in 308 innings compiled a miniscule 1.66 earned run average.

Through the '30s, Giants' manager Bill Terry pitched Hubbell in the first game of doubleheaders and Hal Schumacher in the second—King Carl followed by Prince Hal. The chances of beating one of those two were slim. The chances of beating them both were virtually nil.

In 1933, Hubbell was a solid thirty-year-old pitcher who had yet to win 20 games in a season. Then it all came together, beginning with a 26-inning scoreless streak early in the year. Then in the first game of a July 1 doubleheader against the Cardinals, he pitched a truly remarkable game at the Polo Grounds. After nine innings the score was 0-0. Hubbell had allowed but three hits, while the Cardinals' Tex Carleton had given up only four. They continued to match goose eggs for seven more innings until Carleton was taken out for a pinch hitter.

Jesse Haines retired the Giants in the bottom of the seventeenth, Hubbell mowed the Cardinals down in the top of the eighteenth, and was scheduled to hit fourth in the bottom half. To the delight of the crowd, manager Bill Terry allowed him to hit, with runners on first and second and one out. Although it would be grand to report that Carl got the game-winning hit, he forced Travis Jackson at second, leaving it to the next hitter, Hughie Critz, to drive in the winning run with a liner to center as Carl's teammates mobbed him at second base. Surely, Hubbell's performance that day ranks with the best of all time. Pitching against the future Gashouse Gang, who won the pennant the following year, he allowed six hits, four of which were of the scratch variety, in 18 innings. He struck out 12 and walked none. Twelve innings were perfect and Pepper Martin and Frankie Frisch, two pretty fair ballplayers, were 0 for 14 for the day. Wow!

After pitching the Giants to the pennant in 1933, Carl was not too shabby in the World Series either. In 20 innings against the Washington Senators, he allowed only two unearned runs while winning Games 1 and 4. Game 4 went 11 innings. The Giants pulled ahead by a run in the top of the eleventh, but the Senators came back to load the bases with one out. Bearing down, Hubbell forced pinch-hitter Cliff Bolton to hit into a game-ending double play, giving the Giants a commanding 3-1 lead in games.

Hubbell's most famous feat, of course, occurred in the 1934 All-Star Game, when he struck out Babe Ruth, Lou Gehrig, Jimmie Foxx, Al Simmons, and Joe Cronin in succession. What many do not remember, however, is that Ruth came to bat with runners on first and second and no one out. And with Gehrig at bat, the runners (Charlie Gehringer and Heinie Manush) pulled a double steal. Undaunted, Hubbell got Foxx on three screwballs to end the inning.

Folks also do not remember that Hubbell almost had six in a row. Dickey singled the next inning after Simmons and Cronin had fanned, and then Carl struck out Lefty Gomez to end that inning—six strikeouts of seven batters. Since just about everyone struck out Gomez, however, I guess that doesn't add much to Carl's performance. These other five guys were no slouches at the plate. They have all been in the Hall of Fame for a long time.

Carl peaked again in 1936 and 1937 winning 26 and 22 games. Beginning on July 17, 1936, he won 16 consecutive games through the end of the season. He then began 1937 with eight straight victories to establish a major league record that will likely never be broken, 24 consecutive wins.

I remember that after Hubbell pitched the first game of a double-header he would sit in the clubhouse and ask the clubhouse boy for a couple of scoops of ice cream and a Coca-Cola. Then slowly, very slowly, he mixed the Coca-Cola in the glass with the ice cream until he had just the right consistency. Then contentedly sat and sipped his Coke float, while we were already on the field for the second game. Pretty soon he appeared in the dugout, refreshed and content. I loved being Carl's teammate. He was unassuming, but a terrific competitor who always knew exactly what he was doing on the mound. He had the confidence great players always have, but he was never cocky or arrogant. Carl Hubbell was a fine gentleman.

"They can run like scalded cats." I've never seen a scalded cat run, but that is how Cincinnati Reds manager Bill McKechnie described Paul and Lloyd Waner, and I had enough confidence in Bill to believe him. Paul and Lloyd occupied two of the outfield spots for the Pittsburgh Pirates for much of the late '20s and '30s, but prior to joining Cincinnati in 1939 I had never seen them in action. Thus, McKechnie was briefing me on what to expect prior to our opening game of the season against the Pirates at Crosley Field in Cincinnati. "They are both left-handed batters and can drag bunt or dump the ball down the third base line. They spray the ball all over the field and are really tough to defend." Not only that, I soon learned that the Waners could and did catch anything hit in the air inside any National League ballpark.

Paul was the senior, born in Harrah, Oklahoma, in 1903, three years before Lloyd. On the playing field, they looked, acted, and played like twins. The press dubbed them Big Poison and Little Poison, although in size they were both about five-foot-nine and 150 pounds dripping wet. Paul played in the National League for twenty years and accumulated 3,152 hits while Lloyd had eighteen years of big league service and 2,459 hits. Amazingly, the brothers, both as tough as boot leather, played side by side in the Pittsburgh Pirate outfield for fourteen years.

Paul seemed to get most of the headlines, hitting .380 in 1927 to lead the league in hitting, while Lloyd finished third at .355. Paul also led the league in batting in 1934 with a .364 average, and in 1936 with .373. He finished with a lifetime average of .333. Paul was a friendly sort of guy. On a hot sunny day at Forbes Field in Pittsburgh he'd leg out a triple to the gap and slide into third covered with dust and sweat. While he was dusting himself off, he talked about this or that and I had to move away from him, so strong was the smell of whiskey through his perspiration. I am told that one year Paul announced he was going on the wagon. His batting average was soon hovering around the .250 mark, when, with the aid and consent of his manager, he began imbibing again. Soon his average was back over .300. It was said that he had the sharpest bloodshot eyes in baseball.

The Schenley Hotel was only a block or two from Forbes Field, and it had a cool and comfortable bar where visiting players could sip a beer. Paul was frequently among the visitors with a glass of whiskey in front of him. It never seemed to affect his play, but may eventually have done him in. He died at sixty-two in 1965.

Lloyd, on the other hand, was never seen in the bar and lived to age seventy-six, passing away in 1982. He was my teammate with Cincinnati in 1941, and sitting beside him in the dugout I never smelled anything but shaving lotion. One afternoon, I asked Lloyd how come Paul and he could run so fast. He said it was a matter of life or death. "There's a big Indian

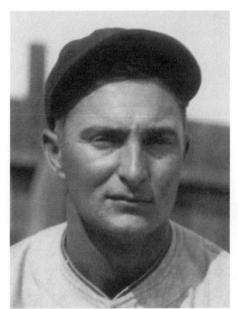

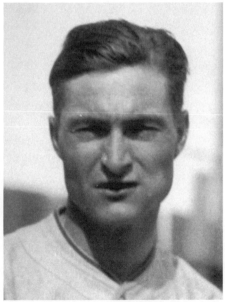

Paul Waner—Big Poison
weighed all of 150 lbs.

Lloyd Waner—Little Poison
topped out at 145.

living outside of Harrah who owned a small farm and grew cantalope, watermelon, eating corn, and tomatoes. We used to walk a mile or so to that farm and steal whatever was in season, and the Indian got sick and tired of our shenanigans. He learned our habits and would lurk in the woods to cut us off, and when he was sure he had us he'd pounce. We'd scatter like a covey of quail with hearts in our mouths. He was a big mean Indian and would have killed us!"

If you ever visit the Baseball Hall of Fame in Cooperstown, look up the Waner brothers. They are both there.

13 A VERITABLE WHO'S WHO OF MANAGING

Casey Stengel, Joe McCarthy, Bucky Harris, Joe Cronin, Connie Mack, Bill McKechnie, and Mel Ott have a couple of things in common. First, they are all in the Baseball Hall of Fame. Second, they all managed one Bill Werber. I played third base or shortstop for these icons of baseball well over a half-century ago. It seems like yesterday. Not all of these gentlemen are in the Hall of Fame for their managing prowess, but most are. Clearly, by Hall of Fame standards, I played for some of the finest managers of all time. In a few cases, I would have been delighted to decline the honor.

If you refer to Charles Dillon Stengel in a conversation, your average listener won't know who you're talking about. If you mention Casey Stengel, however, even many nonfans will recognize the name. Stengel got his nickname from his birthplace, Kansas City, Missouri, where he was born on July 30, 1890. When he first broke into the big leagues, some of his teammates began calling him "K.C." Ernest Thayer's poem "Casey at the Bat" was popular then, and soon the opposition picked up on the "K.C." and began calling him "Casey" whenever he struck out. My association with this garrulous gentleman began in spring training, 1931. The Yankees sent Dixie Walker and me over to Fort Lauderdale to join the Toledo Mud Hens of the American Association, where Mr. Stengel was the manager. Walker was twenty-one and I was twenty-three, but we found ourselves in an assembly of graybeards, and rough ones at that. Casey was forty-one years old, Al DeVormer, Bruno Haas, and Carl Mays were forty, Jack Scott was thirty-nine, Elam Vangilder was thirty-five, and Bevo LeBourveau was thirty-four. Big leaguers on their way down. They smoked, chewed tobacco, drank beer, and spoke profanely—not much inspiration there.

Dixie Walker was a fine hitter who was also a very good center fielder, with an excellent arm and great range. With Toledo, he was saddled on both sides by a couple of plow horses in Bruno Haas and LeBourveau. If a ball was hit on the fly to the outfield and not caught, Walker might as well have "stuck it in his pocket." I played shortstop, and on either side of me were players of modest ability. Despite the level of play that surrounded us, Stengel got on Dixie and me more often than not.

I guess I lost confidence in my manager after his demonstration of how to hook slide, which he performed in the lobby of the Chittenden Hotel in Columbus, Ohio. Casey's execution was all right, but he began his slide on a small scatter rug on a highly polished wood floor and his momentum carried him into a table lamp where he got tangled up with an assortment of wires. I couldn't help laughing at the ridiculous sight, and thereafter I found myself in declining favor with the skipper.

Not long after, I had a bad game against the old Brewers in Milwaukee. I made a couple of errors and I also got thrown out attempting to stretch a double into a triple. (This is "daring on the bases" when you make it, but a "bonehead play" when you do not.) No ballplayer feels good about contributing to a loss, and most will accept constructive criticism leveled in private. On this occasion, Casey chose to voice his criticisms in the clubhouse in front of my twenty-three teammates and in a loud and hostile voice. He accused me of being in the wrong position, throwing to the wrong base, booting easy ground balls, and poor baserunning. The thought occurred to me that not even my father had ever spoken to me so harshly, and here was a relative stranger being verbally abusive. When Casey stopped to catch his breath, I gave him the benefit of my opinion.

On the streetcar from the ballpark back to the hotel, the veteran Johnny Cooney quietly counseled me that no matter what the provocation, it's not a good idea to speak to the manager of a baseball club the way I

Casey Stengel as manager of the Toledo Mud Hens. Not one of my favorites.

had. "He can and will hurt you," Johnny told me. Cooney was right. Stengel refused to play me after that episode.

Luckily for me—but not for the Mud Hens—a number of Ohio banks failed in June. The ballclub and many of the players had money in Security Home Savings in Toledo, and it went broke. The Mud Hens wired the Yankees and asked them for relief for my salary and Walker's. So the Yankees sent Dixie to Toronto and me to Newark in the International League. Casey and his veterans struggled on without the mistakes of youth and finished in the cellar with a record of 68-100, thirty-six-and-a-half games the behind the pennant-winning St. Paul Saints.

So my experience playing for old Casey was not that great. I simply did not like Stengel. He spoke in riddles with that garbled syntax the sportswriters later made to seem brilliant, but that I always thought was a mark of his ignorance. He was hypercritical of his young ballplayers, Walker and me. He was not a teacher, but a faultfinder and a crabby old bore.

Stengel later had huge success with those great Yankee teams of the late '40s, '50s and early '60s, but his big-league managerial record before taking over in New York was dismal. In nine years of managing in the National League with Brooklyn and Boston, he never reached the first division and squeaked out a winning record (77-75 with the '38 Boston Bees) just once. With Boston (which again became the Braves in 1941), he clowned his way to seventh place five years in a row. Only the forlorn Phillies saved him from the basement.

Perhaps his treatment of players improved with the Yankees, but I have my doubts. The Yankees' success in those years had much to do with general manager George Weiss and his legion of scouts who, aided by the Yankee aura and prospects of higher pay and annual World Series checks, assembled teams with tremendous talent. A manager of a great team typically has little to do with the success of the team, other than to not screw up a good thing. Consistent pitching and timely hitting turned Stengel into a genius and convinced the sportswriters of the day that his nonsensical utterances were in fact the learned pontifications of a master.

Joe McCarthy never played an inning of major league baseball, but he managed the New York Yankees to eight pennants in fifteen-plus years, never finishing out of the first division. Overall, he managed twenty-four years in the big leagues, winning 2,126 games, the fourth most in history. I played for "Marse Joe" in spring training in 1931 and 1932 and into the '33 season before I was traded to the Red Sox. To tell the truth, I found him aloof, unfriendly, and sometimes befuddled by drink. For example, on a very cold, raw day in Louisville, Kentucky, on the way north from spring training, he had fortified himself copiously with the hard stuff. As a result, he spent most of the day extolling the virtues of one "Skeeter" Dickey and castigating Ruth, Gehrig, Lazzeri, Combs, and Crosetti, all of whom were wearing the lightweight rubberized tops we called "alligator jackets" under their uniform shirts to keep warm. Several of the stars had made errors and the Yanks were behind.

"Look it 'em," growled McCarthy, "all these high-priced assholes so wrapped up they can't move. The only man on the club is 'Skeeter' Dickey." Way down on the end of the bench with arms exposed to the cold and teeth chattering sat Bill Dickey's eighteen-year-old brother, Skeeter. Of course, young Dickey would have worn an alligator jacket too, plus a blanket, if he could have afforded either. He was freezing on the bench by economic circumstance, not by manly choice.

Like Stengel later, McCarthy was the beneficiary of tremendous talent with the Yankees. General manager Ed Barrow and a first-class scouting staff headed by Paul Krichell were responsible for assembling the great Yankee teams. McCarthy's responsibility was to select the lineup and have Art Fletcher hand it to the umpire before the start of the game. After that, the game was in the hands of Gehrig, Ruth, Dickey, DiMaggio, Lazzeri, Crosetti, Rolfe, Combs, Ruffing, Gomez, and Keller, to mention a few.

In contrast, Bucky Harris was the greatest manager I ever played for. He was a fair to middlin' second baseman for the Washington Senators and became the first "boy manager" in 1924, named to that post by owner Clark Griffith. He did pretty well with it too, leading the Senators to the American League pennant that first year and winning the World Series against the New York Giants in seven games, all at the tender age of 28. After that success he was dubbed "the boy wonder."

I was with the Boston Red Sox when Harris took over as manager in the winter of 1934. His opening remarks to us at the start of spring training in Sarasota, Florida, that March let everyone know we were in for an agreeable summer. "We'll only have one rule this season," he said, "be in bed before twelve o'clock." He added, "Some of you will do some tomcat-ting and I may do some myself, but if you do, get it done before twelve." With that short speech Bucky quickly impressed us as a reasonable person, someone you wanted to play ball for. And that is the way it turned out. We all liked him and worked hard for him. He never faulted aggressive play. If you tried something to win and failed, he would not criticize you.

That spring I played shortstop for the Red Sox in the exhibition games. Before we broke camp to head north, Harris asked me to come up to his room at the Terrace Hotel in Sarasota, where we were training. He and Coach Jack Onslow told me that they were pleased with the work I was doing, that the shortstop job was mine, and that they were going to stick with me. Of course, that made me feel pretty good and I appreciated Bucky's confidence in me.

As the season began, I was sometimes erratic with my throws. Harris still believed I had potential, so he brought Lyn Lary over from the Yankees to play shortstop, moved me to third base, and sold Bucky Walters, who had been playing third, to the Phillies. It was a good move all around. Phils' manager Jimmie Wilson turned Walters into a pitcher and he became an outstanding one. I played third base for the rest of my career, nine years. Walters and I would eventually be teammates on two pennant-winning teams in Cincinnati.

Harris was smart as a briar and had a different set of signals for every batter. The basic signs were simple: if he touched his cap it was bunt; if he touched his shirt it was hit; if he touched his pants it was take. If you were the first batter and he touched his shirt first, you were to hit. If you were the second batter and he touched his cap second, you bunted. Each hitter had but three things to worry about; Harris had twenty-seven.

Later when I played against him, I tried to steal his signs. But he would change them in the middle of a game and I never could figure out what the hell he was doing. Bucky could stand out there giving signals all day long and no one could ever pick them up.

Bucky was not above getting involved in the horseplay that goes on around a ball club. In 1934, we had come off a successful home stand and our spirits were high. It was near the Fourth of July and some of my more exuberant teammates were exploding firecrackers of significant size and noise in our Pullman cars, making the rest of us more than a little jumpy.

After playing an exhibition game in Malone, New York, during the All-Star break, we faced an all-day, all-night train ride to St. Louis. The cars were not air conditioned, except for blocks of ice overhead, so the ballplayers sat around in their BVDs or pajama shorts. A poker game was in progress in the men's washroom involving Bill Cissell, Dusty Cooke, Moose Solters, Roy Johnson, Dusty Rhodes, and Bob Seeds. There was actually more room in the washroom than in the Pullman itself, and the boys had a large piece of cardboard, piled with coins, precariously perched on six pairs of knees.

While the game was going on, Harris came to me and asked, "Bill, you got any of those big blue-nosed matches? I want to have a little fun." So I produced a couple of matches and Bucky stuck them in the end of a cigar. He asked me to light them and then he pulled aside the green curtain to the washroom and tossed the lighted cigar right in the middle of the makeshift table.

Of course, the poker players thought that someone had tossed a lighted firecracker in their midst. They all had the same idea at the same time: get the hell out of here. So the table went flying, as did the cards, the quarters, the fifty cent pieces, and the dollar bills. Six ballplayers came tearing out of the washroom in their underwear, while the money ended up in the wash basins, in spittoons, and all over the floor. Harris was convulsed with laughter. For my part, I just sat quietly reading a magazine. I knew the guys could not get back at Harris, but they sure could get back at me.

Our owner, young Tom Yawkey, was traveling with us on that trip and he got caught up in the merriment, enjoying the devilment and tomfoolery. After a successful series against the Browns, we traveled to Detroit. There, some of us got carried away, tossing lighted Chinese crackers out of seventeenth-floor windows of the Book-Cadillac. The police were called. The next day Mr. Yawkey and Harris called a team meeting and announced that the next big bang would result in a $500 fine. That made the fun much too expensive and put an end to our explosive escapades.

Bucky Harris' relaxed attitude helped build confidence. He knew when to draw the line and, as a result, he could get more out of his players than just about anyone. He managed in the big leagues for twenty-nine years, mostly with bad ball clubs, yet he ranks third all-time with 2,157 wins.

Through an unusual sequence of events the Red Sox had a new manager when I reported to spring training in 1935. He was the twenty-eight year-old future Hall of Fame shortstop Joe Cronin. I was not all that pleased to see him. Cronin played shortstop for Clark Griffith's Washington Senators. Griffith, no doubt remembering the success he had when he chose Harris to manage in 1924, named Cronin in 1933 to succeed the immortal Walter Johnson. As Griffith's second "boy manager," Cronin led the Senators to the American League pennant that year, just as Harris had done nine years earlier. Although they lost the World Series to Bill Terry's Giants in five games, Joe quickly earned a reputation as a top-flight skipper, as well as an outstanding player.

It probably helped that Joe married the boss's neice, Mildred Robertson. Griffith's sister had six children, and when her husband died at an early age, Griffith undertook to raise the kids. He adopted two of them—Thelma and Calvin—and they took the Griffith name. The other four—Mildred, Sherry, Jimmie and Billy—kept the Robertson name. Jimmie and Billy ran the concessions at Griffith Stadium, Sherry played infield for the Senators for ten years during the '40s and early '50s, and Thelma married Joe Haynes, a pitcher for the Senators and White Sox for fourteen years. And Calvin eventually succeeded Mr. Griffith as club president and was responsible for moving the team to Minnesota in 1961.

The press often portrayed Clark Griffith as a penurious sharpie who

Bucky Harris, a very sharp competitor.

paid his players poorly. (Washington was sometimes described as first in war, first in peace, and last in the American League.) The real Griffith was a person of generosity and philanthropy. He was the sole financial support of all the Robertson children and managed to hide most of his charitable activities from public view.

Joe Cronin's time as manager was rather short-lived. After winning the pennant in 1933 by seven games, the Senators slipped to seventh place in 1934, 34 games out of first place. Late in that season, Griffith and Tom Yawkey watched nine innings of baseball together at Griffith Stadium. Mr. Yawkey had money and Mr. Griffith needed money. So when the ballgame was over, the two men had pulled off a blockbuster deal. Cronin was to manage the 1935 Red Sox, while Bucky Harris was to return to Washington to again manage the Senators. The agreement was memorialized by Yawkey tearing off a piece of a brown paper bag and writing on it "I, Thomas A. Yawkey agree to pay $250,000 for the contract and services of Joseph Edward Cronin." One evening after Joe joined our club, my wife Tat and I went to the Cronins' for dinner. Mildred pulled out her scrap book where the torn-off piece of brown paper bag was prominently displayed.

I had two reasons for trepidation when I learned Joe was going to be my manager. First, I really enjoyed playing for Bucky Harris and was sorry to be losing him. Second, Joe and I had had a run-in during the last series between our clubs in 1933, and we had not been on the best of terms since. Washington's pennant that year was largely at the expense of the Red Sox. They really had our number, beating us 18 out of the 22 games we played against them. During that last series, Cronin at one point came out of his dugout hollering some disparaging remarks about the Red Sox. His language was pretty strong and I took offense. So at the end of the inning I waited at third for Cronin to come by on his way to play shortstop and we had words. I told him, "Joe, I'm going to make you pay for that."

We played the Senators on opening day, 1934. Harris told me to get on Cronin while Joe was taking infield before the game. There was lingering animosity between Cronin and Bucky Harris as well. So I got on Joe pretty severely. Everything he did poorly I reminded him of, from infield practice to the end of the game. I had a strong voice and I yelled at him all day from the dugout. In the meantime, I had a great day, going four for four.

Odd thing about this bench jockeying. If you just stay on a guy no matter what he says back to you, just stay on him and stay on him, he will eventually come to you and challenge you. And then you've got him. I stayed on Joe all year long and eventually he challenged me to fight, which is what I wanted because then I knew I had really distracted him.

Joe had a rough year in 1934. The Senators nose-dived, and he himself had a bad thumb that was giving him problems. He hit only .284, a poor mark for him. I might have been a small contributing factor to his troubles. When I came to the ballpark for our last series with the Senators in '34, Harris said to me, "There's your friend out there. Get on him."

But I respected Cronin as a ballplayer, and I decided I was finished. I said to Bucky, "No. I'm going to let the guy alone. I feel sorry for him. He's having a bad year all the way around."

When I read in the Washington *Post* that winter that Cronin had been made the Boston manager, I said to Tat at breakfast, "Well, it doesn't look like we're going to be with the Red Sox much longer." I was wrong. Cronin treated me fairly and I got so I liked the guy. One evening after the season started, Joe asked if we could take a walk together, so we did. He said, "Last year there were some unpleasant things said and some enmities aroused but now we are on the same team together. You are my third baseman and I'd like to get along and be friends with you." I thought that was very decent of him and it was more than acceptable to me. I told Joe that I was very glad to bury the hatchet and pull together to do our best to win. That is why Joe and his wife had Tat and I over to their house for dinner.

Joe Cronin turned out to be a good solid manager, level-headed and a battler. He managed the Red Sox for thirteen years, leading the troops to a pennant in 1946. During his tenure, Boston finished second four times and third once.

We finished a frustrating fourth in 1935, although we had good pitching and decent hitting. It just seemed like a year when the only luck we had was bad. A bizarre play against Cleveland on September 7 in Fenway Park typified our year. We trailed the Indians by four runs in the bottom of the ninth inning, but soon scored two runs and had the bases loaded with no one out. Dusty Cooke was on third, I was on second, and Mel Almada occupied first. That brought up the jut-jawed Cronin, our leading RBI man and one of the top clutch hitters in baseball. The Boston faithful, smelling a comeback victory, sprang to life. Steve O'Neill, the Indians manager, called time to bring in a relief pitcher, Oral Hildebrand. It did not seem to be a very wise choice. Oral had only an average fastball and a mediocre curve. He threw one pitch, a fastball right down the gut, and Cronin crushed a line drive directly to Odell Hale, the Indians' third baseman. Hale lost the ball in the white shirts in the box seats behind the plate, but caught sight of it an instant before it caromed off the side of his head. A direct hit could well have killed him. As luck would have it, the ball deflected straight to shortstop Bill Knickerbocker, who caught it on the fly. Umpire Harry Geisel hollered, "You're out," meaning Cronin. Knickerbocker tossed the ball to Roy Hughes at second and Geisel yelled, "You're out," meaning me since I had started for third at the crack of the bat. Hughes pivoted and fired the ball to Hal Trosky at first to nail Almada, who was desperately trying to get back to first. Waving his arms wildly, Geisel then bellowed, "You're all out." The big crowd was stunned into silence, then erupted with a roar that could be heard for miles. The next day a wag in the Boston *Post* wrote "Cleveland third baseman uses head to win game."

After the 1936 season, the Red Sox traded me to the Athletics for Pinky Higgins in a straight swap of third basemen. In Philadelphia I had the opportunity to play for the venerable Cornelius Alexander McGillicuddy.

He was seventy-five years old, but he wore his years lightly. His pale blue eyes were alert, he strode briskly with a distinctive bounce to his step, and he was sharp as a tack. When I was sitting beside him in the dugout one day in Washington, he spied an elderly gentleman approaching from across the field. "My, my, my," he exclaimed, "That looks like Dr. Morrison. Why, I haven't seen him for over thirty years." And Dr. Morrison it turned out to be.

Known by the press as "the Tall Tactician," Mr. Mack was listed as six-foot-one. He always seemed taller than that to me, probably because of his erect posture and thin frame. Unlike virtually all other managers, he never wore a uniform in the dugout, favoring a three-piece suit with an old-fashioned starched collar shirt. He was always armed with a scorecard, which he waved as a conductor of a symphony waves a baton, moving fielders around and flashing signals to his coaches.

He took great pleasure from baseball, enjoying life to its fullest. In the spring of 1937, the Athletics trained in the high altitude and then clean air of Mexico City. Buoyed by the mild climate and poor opposition from the Mexican clubs, the A's came out of spring training full of self-confidence, and we played over our heads until the Fourth of July. Our lack of talent caught up with us then, and we lost ten of twelve during a homestand. We were happy to leave town on a western road trip to try to get our bearings.

We turned it around quickly in our first game against the White Sox, scoring twelve runs in the first inning. Bob Johnson drove in seven of them with a grand-slam home run and a double. As I came to the dugout after scoring my second run of the inning, Mr. Mack was chuckling.

"What's the matter, Mr. Mack?" I asked.

"My good gracious me," he replied, "isn't this baseball a wonderful game? I never know what to expect. My boys teach me something new every day."

At seventy-five he was still learning and relishing in it.

A more kindly and patient man never lived. No matter how bad the team was playing or how egregious the errors, he never permitted himself to become upset, nor would he utter an oath or raise his voice. And he never upbraided a ballplayer during a game or in front of his teammates for a stupid play. Instead, the next day he would send the clubhouse boy to ask the offending player if he could spare Mr. Mack a moment or two in his office. He would then review the play from the day before, what had gone wrong, and how it should have been handled. He would then say, "If this situation occurs again, would you consider doing it my way?" Since he owned the ball club and paid the salaries, there was little question of compliance with his suggestions. He was, nonetheless, a most reasonable and thoughtful man to deal with.

Although the Tall Tactician was tight with a buck, he would go to great lengths to protect his ballplayers. Then as now, they were young men full of vim and vigor and the joy of living. Occasionally they would tangle with something wearing skirts and have a price to pay. During my time with the Athletics, several of my teammates managed to contract gonorrhea and got so sick that they could not play. Mr. Mack covered for the players with the press and, if they were married, with their wives. I always suspected that he made them pay when it came contract time.

Mr. Mack had a rare ability to recognize talent well before it flowered. If he saw a nascent ability, he often would play young ballplayers and let them learn through experience. Early in his career he had great success with collegians such as "Gettysburg Eddie" Plank, Columbia's Eddie Collins, and "Colby Jack" Coombs, who was later my coach at Duke. Although he also fielded a number of college players who did not pan out, he remained partial to them if he believed they had some talent.

In 1938, Mr. Mack signed Sam Chapman, who had been an All-American halfback at the University of California at Berkeley. Sam was big and strong, but was initially pretty clumsy as a ballplayer. Shortly before he was to join us, Mr. Mack asked me to look after the rookie "to see that he gets off to a good start and stays with the right attitude."

In his first game, against Cleveland at League Park, Sam got his feet tangled and let a routine fly ball hit by Earl Averill drop with men on base, costing us a couple of runs and ultimately the game. Harry Kelley was pitching for us and when the inning was over he threw his glove against the dugout wall and let loose a tirade against "lousy college ballplayers and ignorant managers." It was ugly. Mr. Mack sat quietly composed throughout the harangue and never responded, letting the fire die of its own accord.

Harry Kelley was by no means a bad fellow. He was a thirty-two-year-old veteran who had toiled in the minor leagues for more than a decade before getting his shot in the majors. He had worked like a dog to get to the Athletics and he believed he deserved more than ineptitude in the field. Mr. Mack understood this and just kept quiet. Incidentally, he was correct about Sam Chapman, too. Sam went on to give yeoman's service to the Athletics for eleven years.

Was Connie Mack a great manager? It's hard to say, because he was the owner and had to be primarily a businessman. To subsist economically he dismantled both his great championship teams. He survived the many lean years because he owned the ballclub. If he fired himself, he would simply have had another salary to pay. Overall, Mr. Mack managed the Athletics for fifty-three years, winning more games, 3,731, than anyone in history, but losing more, 3,948, too. He was a fine man, and although we got into a serious tussle over money, I am glad to have had the opportunity to play for him.

When we reached an impasse over my salary shortly before the 1939 season, I was sold out of the league to the Cincinnati Reds. It turned out to be a great move for me. Not only did I join a contender (the Reds had finished fourth in 1938, only six games behind the pennant-winning Cubs), but I had the chance to play for another fine skipper, Bill McKechnie. By then McKechnie was fifty-four and had managed seventeen big league seasons, winning the pennant and a seven-game World Series with the Pittsburgh Pirates in 1925 and leading the St. Louis Cardinals to

Bucky Walters and Bill McKechnie.
A 27 game winner and a Hall of Fame manager.

the 1928 pennant before they were swept by the powerful Yankees. He had endured some lean years with the Boston Braves in the '30s and had learned to accept the gristle with the meat. The press often referred to McKechnie as "Deacon," although whether from a church affiliation or his normally sober mien, I'm not sure. He never cursed and he was a calm customer who steered a steady course through victory or defeat, never getting too high or too low.

McKechnie stressed fundamentals and conditioning. In spring training we practiced bunting every time at bat. He was a very good strategist and was patient with his players. He was also thoughtful and generous. When the ball club was playing well, he'd pay out of his own pocket to have a tub of beer on ice in the clubhouse after the game. I was not a beer drinker, but my locker was near the entrance to the little room where McKechnie and his coaches, Hank Gowdy and Jimmie Wilson, dressed. Bill encouraged me to have a bottle to replace some of the fluids we lost during the game. The team appreciated the beer, and we all thought it was an especially generous gesture inasmuch as he didn't drink himself. On train rides McKechnie would chat with us about hunting and fishing or life in general. He stayed down on our level all the time. Whatever mistake a player made during a game, Bill always handled it the same way Mr. Mack did. He never upbraided anyone, but he'd talk to us man-to-man afterward.

Only once in three years did I see him angry. On the Fourth of July, 1939, we had a two-game lead over the Cardinals and we seesawed all the long hot summer. It was a harrowing, pressure-packed time and the tension and fatigue began to tell. On September 26 the Cardinals came to Cincinnati for a four-game series that would decide the pennant. We had a two-game lead and needed only to split the series to clinch first place. We had a pitcher named Whitey Moore, a sturdy strong-armed reliever without a brain in his head, but so good-humored that he was a favorite of his teammates. On the day before the Cardinals arrived, McKechnie stopped him as he was leaving the clubhouse and said, "Whitey, the Cardinals are coming to town tomorrow and it's going to be a tough series."

"Yeah Bill, I know."

"I may have to use you in all four ballgames, so I want you to go home and get your rest."

"Yeah Bill, I will. I'll be ready."

The next morning's Cincinnati *Enquirer* greeted us with the headline: "Reds' Pitcher Escapes Death." It seems that Whitey had been drinking at a nightclub and had consumed enough whiskey to think a railroad track was a highway. He had narrowly missed being hit by a late express train. He ended up in jail, where the police pumped his stomach and called McKechnie at two in the morning to come get him. We expected that our pregame meeting, when McKechnie customarily went over the opposition's hitters, would be a classic, and we were not disappointed. We all loved Whitey, but we expected the house to fall in on him. McKechnie started calmly enough, but soon lost his composure. "Dammit Whitey, why'd you do it?" "I don't know, Bill. I dunno what happened. I thought it was a road."

"I ought to fine you $500 and I would if you were making any money." "You oughta make it $1,000, Bill," was Whitey's only reply.

That conversation was the only time I ever heard McKechnie swear. The effect was truly comical. Some of the guys had their heads in their lockers with towels stuffed in their mouths to stifle their laughter. The episode served to loosen us up and we beat the Cardinals in the first two games to clinch the first pennant for Cincinnati since the 1919 Black Sox scandal. Whitey did not have to pitch, but Bill's hair turned a shade grayer.

McKechnie was a very loyal and patient manager and although those are very commendable qualities, sometimes they worked against him. We followed our 1939 pennant with an even stronger performance in 1940, winning by twelve games and the World Series in seven over Detroit. During spring training the following year, Paul Derringer, Ival Goodman, and Frank McCormick came to me and said, "We can't win this year with the players Bill has in the lineup. Why don't you talk to him?" A few of the regulars had lost just enough that they could no longer perform at the level we needed if we were going to remain the best team in the league.

My response was, "Why don't you talk to him yourselves?"

They said, "Well, he would listen to you."

I was reluctant to do it but we were playing the Tigers in Crosley Field in the last exhibition game before the regular season started the following day. I was a baserunner on third, McKechnie was the third-base coach, and the Tigers were changing pitchers, so we had a little break in the game. I said, "Bill, the fellows don't believe we can win with the lineup we've got." He said, "What's the complaint?" I mentioned a couple of regulars who had been fine ballplayers but seemed to be slipping. Bill had such an even disposition that he did not take offense. Instead he said,

"Maybe they're right, but these guys have performed well for me in the past and I'm going to have to stay with them."

He did stay with them, and by the Fourth of July we were far behind the Brooklyn Dodgers. Bill then made the changes the guys were suggesting before the season and we played the Dodgers and the second-place Cardinals even the rest of the way. McKechnie certainly knew more baseball than his players and was a better manager than any of us could have been. In this instance at least, he was too slow to replace some players who had lost a step or two simply because he was so devoted to those of us who had won for him. But Bill McKechnie was a class act. He was most deserving of his 1962 election to the Hall of Fame.

After 1941 I had hoped to retire, but the Giants persuaded me to play third base for them for a year. There I met Mel Ott, a great ballplayer who had been named by Giant's owner Horace Stoneham to succeed Bill Terry as manager. Ott had come up to the Giants in 1926 at the tender age of seventeen, and for the next twenty-two years plied his trade with the best of them. The bright lights of New York never fazed this lad, nor did the greatly deserved adulation he received affect the size of his hat.

John McGraw, legendary manager of the Giants, had had the good sense not to change Ott's peculiar batting style, which incorporated a lift of his front leg more than half a century before that became a common practice among players. Mel responded with 511 career home runs and a lifetime .304 batting average. In his fourteen or so prime years, his average was considerably higher, and he drove in 100 or more runs nine times.

Mel was thirty-three years old when I joined the Giants and already a veteran of sixteen big league seasons. For all of that time he had been one of the guys, always involved in the escapades that were part of life with a baseball team. This put Mel at a real disadvantage when it came to exacting discipline, and he was such a nice man that he did not attempt it. He was always pleasant and never fussed at or scolded a player. Sometimes a manager, to be effective, has to get on his players, but Mel couldn't do it.

Ott was a player-manager and had two very savvy coaches, Dolf Luque and Bubber Jonnard. I've already mentioned these two and their love of hot crawfish. Each was delightful in his own way and more than competent to assist in running a game. They took quite a load off of Mel's shoulders and allowed him to continue to play right field and produce at bat. Mel slammed 30 home runs and drove in 93 runs, and we finished in third place with a very respectable 85-67 record. We were never really in contention, though, and we finished twenty games behind the pennant-winning Cardinals and eighteen games behind the second-place Dodgers.

Although I retired from baseball after the 1942 season to repair my injured toe and devote myself full-time to the life insurance business, Ott continued to manage the Giants until midway through the 1948 season. The club dropped to the cellar in 1943, then struggled through the rest of his tenure, finishing as high as fourth in 1947. Mel Ott was a great ballplayer, a good friend, and a wonderful person. He knew the game, but he was just too nice a guy to really succeed at running a ballclub. He was elected to the Hall of Fame in 1951 but died tragically in a car accident in 1958. He was only 49.

These men were imperfect, as we all are. Bucky Harris and Bill McKechnie were my personal favorites. I learned from all of them, however. Looking back more than 60 years ago, I am proud to have played for all of these great baseball men. Stengel, McCarthy, Cronin, Harris, Mack, McKechnie, and Ott. How fortunate I was!

14 SOME PRETTY FAIR TIGERS

The Detroit Tigers were one of the strongest teams of the Depression Era, winning three pennants and a world championship, and finishing second twice. They were lead by remarkable ballplayers like Hank Greenberg, Charlie Gehringer, and Mickey Cochrane, and I had the distinction and challenge of playing against them for most of a decade.

Greenberg was one of the finest ballplayers of his generation. The son of Romanian immigrants, he could have been the Jewish star Giants manager John McGraw was always looking for. But McGraw passed on Greenberg after a tryout, thinking the six-foot-four Hank was too clumsy and too uncoordinated. The Yankees were interested, but Hank turned down their offer because Lou Gehrig was entrenched at first base. He signed with the Tigers in 1930. Hank broke into the big leagues in 1933 and became a star in 1934, hitting .339 with 26 homers and 139 RBIs as Detroit won the American League pennant. The Tigers repeated in 1935, and Hank was the league's Most Valuable Player with two-thirds of a triple crown—36 homers and 170 runs batted in. He recovered from a broken wrist to hit .337 and drive in an astounding 183 runs in 1937.

When Greenberg came to the big leagues in 1933, he took at lot of vicious antisemitic bench jockeying. First base in Detroit was forty feet from the visitors' dugout. Opponents used to really lay it on him, shouting mean, nasty epithets. He was not the only Jewish ballplayer of his day, but he was the best, and he was tough and aggressive. His attitude inspired retaliation, but the more a team got on him, the more he bore down.

In 1938, Hank's disposition worked against him. He had a great year and made a serious run at Babe Ruth's record of 60 home runs in a season. With about five games left in the season, he had slugged 58 round trippers to tie Jimmie Foxx for the most homers by a righthanded hitter. I was with the Athletics when we came into Detroit at the end of the season. Mr. Mack told us in a pregame meeting that Greenberg would be over-anxious trying to break Ruth's record. He instructed our pitchers not to throw anything near the plate. Hank got nothing good to hit for the whole series, and was so impatient that he flailed away at bad balls.

Hank and I were on friendly terms and were once involved in a funny incident during the game that home plate umpire Harry Geisel finally called when he slipped in the rain and the mud. In an early inning with Greenberg on first base, Gee Walker lined a hit to center field. Olympic athlete Jesse Hill, who was the A's centerfielder, instinctively raced in to field the ball on the bounce. But it hit a large puddle and stopped. Hill picked it up and threw to me at third. Normally, Hank would have made third standing up, but because of the conditions, he had to round second very gingerly to avoid slipping in the mud. When he came into third, Del Baker, the third-base coach, gave him the signal to slide.

Greenberg slid right through me on the slick surface, and carried me into Baker. Hank was on the bottom, I was on top of him, and Baker was on top of me. I didn't have the ball, but I extricated myself and tried to find it. Baker was yelling to Greenberg, "Go on home! Go on home!"

Hank said, "No, he knows where the ball is. He knows where the ball is." But I didn't know where the ball was. Finally, the base umpire saw the ball, pointed, and said, "There it is. There it is, rolled up in the mud." So I picked up the muddy ball and Hank stayed on third base. Later, Hank sent a picture of the play to me and signed it "Here's mud in your eye—Hank Greenberg."

Greenberg earned his second MVP award in 1940, hitting .340 and leading the league in doubles (50), home runs (41), and RBIs (150). Then

Hank Greenberg—toughness in the face of adversity.

a bachelor, he was one of the first big leaguers inducted into military service, only nineteen games into the 1941 season. He was discharged two days before Pearl Harbor, and immediately reenlisted as a officer candidate in the Air Corps, where he served with distinction in the Far East. Hank lost four-and-a-half seasons of baseball when he was in his early 30s, but never complained. He was a successful baseball executive after his retirement and later had a fine career as an investment banker.

Greenberg's longtime teammate Charlie Gehringer was one of the finest second basemen ever to play the game. The two of them were called "the G-Men of Detroit." Dependable and undemonstrative, Gehringer was known as "the Mechanical Man." Teammate Roger "Doc" Cramer said, "You wind him up opening day and forget him." Tiger manager Mickey Cochrane once said, "Charlie says `hello' on opening day, `goodbye' on closing day, and in between hits .350." Lefty Gomez expressed a similar sentiment when he said, "He hits .354 on opening day and .354 the rest of the season." He was certainly one of the best ballplayers I ever played against. He did not have much to say, just went about his business in a most efficient manner. He was a smooth fielder with great range, leading the league's second basemen in fielding percentage nine times, and leading or tying for the lead in assists seven times.

Charlie was also one of the top hitters of his day, compiling a lifetime .320 average. He led the league in his MVP year of 1937 with a .371 average, and he stroked more than 200 hits and drove in more than 100 runs seven times. He had great bat control and rarely struck out. In his sixteen full seasons, his strikeout total ranged from 16 to 42. Gehringer often deliberately took one or two strikes before swinging. When asked why he always took the first pitch, he said, "So the pitcher can start off even with me." It was always a mistake to relax defensively because he was behind in the count. He was only going to swing once and when he did he usually hit the ball with authority. Early in my career, I hit a ball up the middle against the Tigers that I knew was a basehit. I was young and foolish and

Charlie Gehringer—a quiet man but what a ballplayer.

I did not get into high gear from the very start. Gehringer went over almost behind second base and made a backhand grab of the ball, slid with his foot, and threw me out at first. When he did that, I said to myself, "That will never happen to me again." From then on, any ball that I hit in his general area, I put on the flag and ran as hard as I could from the get-go. He was so smooth he seemed almost motionless out there, but he covered a lot of territory.

As good a fielder as Gehringer was, I discovered that he had a flaw upon which I capitalized a number of times. He always positioned himself in front of the bag to receive the catcher's throw on attempted steals of second. That meant he had to catch the ball and reach back to tag the runner, so I only gave him the toe of my shoe on the outside of the bag when I was stealing. Many times he could not reach me, so I stole more bases against Detroit than against any other team in the American League. I never brought this to his attention and never mentioned it to anyone to this day. He was a far better ballplayer than I was and this is like a peasant criticizing the king. That was the only flaw I ever saw in his game.

I did catch Gehringer with his pants down on that one one occasion in Boston in 1934, when I took second on a walk when I realized he wasn't paying attention. The Tigers won the game in extra innings, with Schoolboy Rowe notching his sixteenth consecutive victory to tie the American League record. Schoolboy led the Tigers to the pennant that year with a 24-8 record. During the World Series against the Cardinals, he was giving a radio interview when all of a sudden he blurted out to his sweetheart the temporarily famous line, "How'm I doin', Edna?" All the next season, when Schoolboy pitched against us we shouted after about every pitch, "How'm I doin', Edna? How'm I doin', Edna?"

Tiger player-manager Mickey Cochrane was one of two marvelous American League catchers during my era. Bill Dickey of the Yankees was the other. Two superb catchers performed in the National League as well, Gabby Hartnett of the Cubs and Ernie Lombardi of the Reds. I played with and against all four and they were tough cookies. No one could throw a ball harder or more accurately than Lombardi. No player generated more respect than Bill Dickey for his clutch play defensively and at the plate. For geniality and maintenance of team morale there was Gabby, who also was a fine performer in the pinch. His "Homer in the Gloamin'" on September 28, 1938, against Pirate relief ace Mace Brown, with darkness and haze enveloping Wrigley Field propelled the Cubs to the pennant.

And then there was Mickey Cochrane, called "Black Mike" in deference to his competitive nature. Mickey's biggest asset, among several, was his aggressiveness. When the umpire yelled "play ball," you could see him bow his neck and take on that combative attitude. He was on the ballfield to beat you. His attitude affected whoever was pitching. If George Earnshaw seemed a little lackadaisical, Cochrane would fire the ball back at him hard enough to knock him off the mound. His leadership was infectious and inspired his whole ball club.

Schoolboy Rowe—
"How am I doin', Edna?"

Mickey Cochrane—Black Mike
had a soft spot.

For the dominant Athletics of 1929, 1930, and 1931, Mickey was the spark that kept their fire burning. In those years he hit .331, .357, and .349, Brobdingnagian results for any wearer of the "tools of ignorance." His life-time .320 average is the best ever for a catcher. Agile and quick behind the plate, he let very few errant pitches, high, wide or in the dust, get past his glove. He was faster afoot than any of his infielders, save Jimmie Foxx, and sometimes batted in the leadoff position. You had to react quickly defensively or he would beat your throw to first base. He was a hustler.

Mickey, along with Lefty Grove, absolutely hated to lose. Longtime A's teammate Doc Cramer once said, "Lose a one-to-nothing game and you didn't want to get into the clubhouse with Grove and Cochrane. You'd be ducking stools and gloves and bats, and whatever else would fly."

Mr. Mack sold Mickey to Detroit in 1934, where he managed and caught, hit .320 and brought "Tiger Town" its first pennant in many a year. Along the way he won his second MVP award. He led the Tigers to another pennant and to a World Series triumph in 1935, batting .319. After a second-place finish in 1936, tragedy struck the next spring, when an errant pitch from Yankee Bump Hadley fractured his skull. Mickey was rushed to a hospital in critical condition and was close to death for several days. He recovered to manage the Tigers again, but his playing days were over, and in August, 1938, he was fired.

I will always have a soft spot in my heart for Mickey Cochrane because of an incident in 1934. He was on first base in a game at Fenway Park against my Red Sox. The Tiger batter singled to right and Cochrane rounded second and headed for third under a full head of steam. He arrived at third with the throw from right field, which put me blocking his path in an exposed position. The runner is entitled to the bag and Mickey had every right to come in with spikes flying and knock me into the box seats. Fortunately, Cochrane the competitor also had compassion. He slid past me and grabbed the bag with his hand, avoiding any contact. I never thanked him, but I have always remembered how he avoided injuring me.

15 THE THUMPER

He came up in 1939, a gangly kid, six-foot-three and possibly 170 pounds. He wore the bottom of his baggy baseball pants down around his ankles, so who knows what kind of legs he had. He couldn't run. But his eyesight was sharp as a falcon's and his hands and arms were strong. Not only that, they were synchronized and struck with the speed of a cobra. The results were most impressive. Ted Williams could hit. His lifetime batting average of .344 is sixth all-time and only Babe Ruth has a higher slugging percentage than his .634. If he had not lost almost five years of his baseball prime to service in World War II and the Korean War, he would own a bunch more records and have staked an even more undisputed claim to the title of best hitter ever.

His hometown San Diego Padres signed him off the sandlots, and at seventeen he was holding his own in the very fast Pacific Coast League. After a year and a half there, the Red Sox bought him and sent him to the Minneapolis Millers of the American Association. He tore up the league, leading in batting average (.366), home runs (43), RBIs (142), and runs (130). In other words, not only did he win the Triple Crown, he won the Quadruple Crown.

With these credentials, Ted reported to the Red Sox spring training camp in Sarasota, Florida, in 1939 with more than a little ballyhoo. He did not disappoint. That was my first year with Cincinnati and we trained in nearby Tampa. We played the Red Sox fifteen or sixteen times in Florida and on the way north in places like Charleston, South Carolina; Florence,

Alabama; Durham, North Carolina; and Charleston, West Virginia.

In 1939, the Reds won the National League pennant on the strength of our pitching. Bucky Walters won 27, high for both leagues, and Paul Derringer 25. Our others were pretty good, too: Jim Turner, Junior Thompson, Lee Grissom, Whitey Moore, and Johnny Vander Meer. Someone must have forgotten to tell Williams how good our pitching was. He murdered them all.

Our last exhibition game against the Red Sox was in Charleston. Derringer, in frustration, threw a very high, slow ball to Ted and hollered loud enough to be heard all over the ballpark, "Hit that, you son of a bitch." Williams took a couple of hitches with his bat and, using his own power, hit a towering fly that bounced off the right-field wall for a double.

The first personal contact that I had with Ted was in the Boston Pullman car on our way north. The Red Sox had the three cars ahead of us as we rattled along up the Atlantic Coast through South Carolina. I was reading in one of the Reds' cars after dinner when Tom Daly sat down beside me. Tom was a coach with the Sox and had been our bullpen catcher when I played there. His face was the map of Ireland and he was full of all kinds of laughter and yarns and tricks to pull guys out of their gloomy moods. Although he had only a .239 lifetime average as a backup catcher, as a morale-builder on a ballclub, he batted a thousand.

Daly had perfected a gimmick of the kind that ballplayers loved. In his coat pocket he carried a number of buckshot pellets and several bamboo slivers of considerable tensile strength. He would place a shot between his teeth and then flick it with a bamboo sliver. Tom was so accurate that he could sit in an aisle seat of a Pullman dining car and flick a buckshot into the water glass of a diner across the aisle. Said diner, noting the buckshot, would ask the waiter for a fresh glass of water, only to find shortly thereafter another shot in the fresh glass. At the movies, Tom would find a seat a couple of rows behind a bald-headed man and bounce pellets off his noggin. Invariably the poor man would move. Funny to say, but this kind of juvenile activity always seemed to produce more base hits. When I was with the Red Sox, Tom gave me some of his shot and bamboo slivers and I practiced long and hard, but with no appreciable results.

On this occasion, however, Tom had something else in mind. He sat down beside me, bubbling with anticipation, and said, "We've got it all set up for you to pluck a pigeon with that ghost story of yours."

"Who's the victim?" I asked.

"Ted Williams," he responded. "He's stretched out in a berth reading a western but I'll get him to join us and I know that he'll react." So Daly returned to the Red Sox car and after a few minutes I followed him. "The Kid" was stretched out in a made-up berth on the right, and across the aisle at a card table sat Daly and Roger Cramer, facing each other. I sat down beside Daly and after a bit of conversation, they coaxed Ted into taking the seat facing me to hear my unusual yarn.

My story was made to order for a gullible young rookie. It revolved around a supposed initiation stunt conducted by twelve members of my own Sigma Chi fraternity. The dozen had brought two pledges to an eerie, abandoned old mill on a dark and stormy night for initiation rites. One pledge, given only matches, was sent to the black interior of the mill with instructions to explore every nook and cranny. A few minutes later, the second pledge was sent inside with the same instructions. After the failure of either to reappear after a long wait, the alarmed Sigma Chi's entered the decaying old building to look for the pledges. Footprints were visible on a dust-covered stairway and the men followed them to the second floor where the trail led to a door ajar on rusty and creaky hinges. When they peered inside the door with their flashlights, they saw a most horrifying sight. One pledge, in a maddened frenzy, was beating the second boy with his own bloodied arm, which had been ripped from its socket.

Needless to say, I had Ted's full attention. Continuing on, I described the dreadful trauma from which each Sigma Chi suffered as a result of that ghastly night at the old mill. In each of the eleven years since that terrible

Ted Williams, the Splendid Splinter. The kid could hit like no other.

night one of the twelve fraternity men had gone mad. Then, with a maniacal, distorted face, and pointing my fingers toward his eyes, I lunged at Ted and screamed, "This is the twelfth year and I am the twelfth man!"

Ted bolted out of his Pullman seat and began to pummel me with both fists as I quickly ducked and put my arms over my head. I'm glad he didn't have a bat handy, or he would have beat a tattoo on my skull. Ted might have been a little gullible, but there was nothing wrong with his reflexes. After that prank, our paths did not cross again except for spring training games the next couple of years. That was all right with me, considering the way he mauled our pitching staff.

A number of years later after my playing days, but while Ted was still active, I was standing on a street corner in Chicago waiting for the light to change when Ted pulled up in his his car. He hollered for me to come get in. He then circled around the block, parked the car, and we went into a restaurant to share a Coke. We talked about hunting and fishing, since I had just returned from shooting canvasbacks up on Lake Winnipegosis in Manitoba and Ted was an avid (and outstanding) hunter and fisherman. On subsequent accidental meetings, our topics of conversation were similar: hunting, fishing, and baseball—matters of common interest.

In the late '70s, I was visiting my friend Dick Locker, who had served with Ted as a Marine combat pilot in Korea and remained a fast friend. When Ted learned that Tat and I were at Islamorada, in Florida, he invited the Lockers and us over to dinner and cooked us some steaks. Dick had told Ted that I was a bit on the deaf side, but after a couple of martinis, he became confused and thought it was Tat who had trouble hearing. As he told a story during dinner, he leaned halfway across the table, look Tat in the eye, and bellow, "Did you hear what I said?" Yes, she heard him okay. I did, too, and we all had a great time.

Ted now lives with a caretaker and a Dalmatian named Slugger in a big house on a hilltop near Hernando, Florida, shaded by giant water oaks dripping with moss. Close by is the very handsome Ted Williams Museum with a Hitters' Hall of Fame and much of Ted's baseball memorabilia. Ted has had a serious stroke and needs the aid of a walker, but there is nothing wrong with his mind, or for that matter, his voice. He still fills a room merely by entering it. Indeed his resonant, distinctive voice fills it before he enters.

On our most recent visit, we met a young girl who was leaving as we arrived. She had suffered a serious head injury in a car accident. Ted had met her in the hospital while he was recovering from his stroke and they had become fast friends. He had offered her his whirlpool, and she and her physical therapist came several days a week. Also at Ted's house were guests from Minnesota, an elderly man and his middle-aged daughter. The man was a buddy from World War II—an aviation mechanic who maintained the planes Ted flew. They came for a visit every year.

Ted was delighted to see all of us and had obviously been looking forward to our arrival. We sat down to a sumptuous dinner and talked baseball and the old days for several hours. He seemed to really enjoy being with another old ballplayer and even remarked that he appreciated my "banty rooster" style of play. When it came time to leave, a sadness overtook us. Ted told me to come back soon, but we both knew that probably would not happen. I was nearing 90, and Tat and I were about to move to Charlotte, North Carolina, to be nearer our children. We knew we woudn't be traveling much anymore and we knew that Ted wouldn't, either. So we said our farewells, two old ballplayers nearing the sunset.

16 WORLD CHAMPIONS

In my three years with Cincinnati, the Reds won two National League pennants and one World Series. When I joined the team in the spring of 1939 the only person I knew was Bucky Walters, my teammate and friend from the 1933 Red Sox. But I didn't have to know any of the other players to understand quickly that we had guys with ability and character. We were playing baseball for a living, we had a good team of good people, and we won. What could be more fun?

My teammates on those Reds ball clubs were, of course, just as human as the rest of the population, with their strange quirks and traits. Some were better ballplayers than they were men, but they were pretty good men as well.

Frank McCormick and the Jungle Club

I always believed in playing ball with all-out effort, pep, and hustle. When I joined the Reds I started firing the ball around the infield after an out or a strikeout, instead of just lobbing it. It was a small thing, but pretty soon Billy Myers at shortstop and Lonnie Frey at second were zinging the ball around, too. Lonnie had liver-colored birthmarks over much of his body and he was lithe and graceful, so with typically crude ballplayer's humor I began calling him the Leopard. Myers wanted to know what I was going to call him so I told him, "You're the Jaguar and I'm the Tiger." To keep each other and anybody else alert we would holler, "Bounce around on the balls of your feet like a jungle cat." And so the Jungle Cats were born. We knew that our hustling, scrapping attitude would help us win, because we had a lot of talent to go with it.

Pretty soon Frank McCormick, our first baseman, wanted to know when he could get in the Jungle Club. I said, "To hell with you Frank. You don't hustle all the time."

McCormick came from New York City and was an outstanding hitter. He was six-foot-four and could hit screaming line drives all over the field. In 1938 he had batted .327 and led the league with 209 base hits. He had smacked 40 doubles and driven in 106 runs, even though he hit only five home runs. Frank had amazing bat control. In 1938, he struck out only seventeen times in 640 official trips to the plate. Frank was a fine fellow with a pleasant disposition and was devoted to his wife, Vera. He was a good gloveman around first, but he was almost exclusively interested in hitting. Although he was potentially the best player on the club, he didn't always play heads-up ball or do the little things that help win ball games.

But Frank really wanted in the Jungle Club. He said to me, "If I hustle good for a week will you take me in?" I said, "A week! Maybe if you hustle for a month we might consider it."

Frank was already hitting, and now he began to hustle as well, stretching singles into doubles and bouncing around first base like the big cat that he was. Almost every day he would ask, "Did I hustle good? When am I getting into the Jungle Club?" A few weeks later we were in Boston when Frank had a big day with several hits and runs batted in. We were sharing a taxicab back to the Copley Plaza Hotel after the game and Frank again asked, "When am I getting into the Jungle Club?" So I said, "Frank, you've really been hustling and you have earned the right to come into the Jungle Club."

He said, "What are you going to call me? Are you going to call me the Wildcat?" I said, "When we get to the hotel, join us in the Merry-Go-Round Room and buy us each a beer and we'll give you your name." So we sat in a booth and Frank bought us beers and then asked, "Now what are you going to call me? You're going to call me the Wildcat, aren't you?" I said, "Frank, we've had a meeting and we have decided to call you the Hippopotamus." Frank was crushed and hurt. He said, "Then I don't want to join the Jungle Club. I'm not going to be the Hippopotamus. I want to be the Wildcat." I said, "Frank, calm down. You are the Wildcat and you are a Wildcat."

Frank jumped up from the table and went into the lobby of the hotel where players were still milling around after coming in from the ballpark and announced, "I'm in the Jungle Club and they've named me the Wildcat." Then he saw our manager, Bill McKechnie, and he ran over and told him the same thing. "I'm in the Jungle Club. They call me the Wildcat."

The Jungle Club may seem silly, but it helped our infield defense stay on its toes and certainly contributed to our success. We came up with all sorts of new defensive strategies on the long train rides or in hotel lobby bull sessions in the evening after day games. We Jungle Clubbers thought

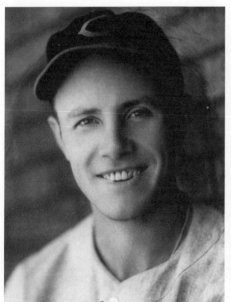

Lonnie Frey and Billy Myers—charter members of the Jungle Club and a great pair up the middle.

and talked baseball all the time.

As for McCormick, he went on to hit .332 and lead the league with 209 hits for the second year. He drove in 128 runs to lead the league in that category as well. He was again almost impossible to strike out, fanning seventeen times in 670 at bats. Although Bucky Walters narrowly beat him out for the 1939 Most Valuable Player award, he would win it with another banner year in 1940 when we went on to the world championship.

The Schnozz—Ernie Lombardi

Our catcher is in the Hall of Fame. Ernie Lombardi, a big, easygoing guy from the Bay Area, was a superb hitter and defensive catcher, exceptional in every area save foot speed. In 1938, he won the National League MVP award and the batting title with a .342 average. This was a tremendous accomplishment, considering that he was so slow afoot, and was such a dead-pull hitter that the third baseman and shortstop played back on the outfield grass against him. His lifetime batting average in seventeen big league seasons was .306 and he remains the only catcher to win two batting titles.

Ernie was six-foot-three and at least 230 pounds. Pitching to him was like throwing to a warehouse behind the plate. Our staff liked throwing to him. He knew the opposition's strengths and weaknesses and called a great game. He was a shrewd operator. Lombardi could throw better than anybody—anybody. When an opposing runner tried to steal third, I knew we had an out when I saw Ernie's arm drop because the ball would always arrive on target and light as a feather.

Friends called him "Lom" or "Schnozz," the later because of the prominence of his nose. Lom was a memorable snorer as well. He was so loud that we consigned him on Pullmans to the press car, which was separate from ours. That gesture may not have done much for our relations with the media, but at least we were assured of a decent night's sleep. Unfortunately, Ernie is remembered for his famous "snooze" in the final

Ernie Lombardi—amarvelous catcher, superb hitter and great guy.

game of the 1939 World Series as much as for his Hall of Fame career. It happened in the fourth and, it turned out, final game. We had taken a 4-2 lead into the ninth inning but the Yankees rallied to tie us, 4-4. We failed to score in our half, sending the game into extra innings.

Bucky Walters, pitching in relief of Derringer, walked Frank Crosetti to start the tenth. Red Rolfe sacrificed Crosetti to second and the Yankees had two on when shortstop Billy Myers fumbled Charlie Keller's grounder. Joe DiMaggio singled through the infield to right, scoring Crosetti with the go-ahead run. The ball somehow ran up Ival Goodman's right arm, getting by him. Keller, a rock solid 185 pounds, raced around the bases and headed home, crashing full tilt into Lombardi just as the ball arrived from Goodman.

The impact stunned Ernie and knocked the ball a few feet away. DiMaggio, rounding second, halted and then took off for third when he saw the ball jolted loose. I was glad to see Joe coming because I was sure Lom would jump up, grab the ball and throw to me at third to nail him. Ernie, however, remained prone on the ground while DiMaggio made third. Then Yankee third base coach Art Fletcher waved Joe home. Ernie cleared his cobwebs just as DiMaggio reached the plate, found the ball and, too late, lunged at Joe sliding by.

We failed to score in the bottom of the tenth, giving the Yanks the game, 7-4, and a Series sweep. Although much was made of "Lombardi's swoon" in the press, the truth of the matter was that it had made no difference in the outcome of the game. DiMaggio's hit had scored the winning run. His run simply made the final score 7-4 rather than 6-4.

One afternoon in the dugout the following year I asked Ernie, "Lom, what ever happened to you last year at home plate?" "I don't know, Bill," was his simple response. He never tried to alibi or make excuses, just took the negative press like a man. It certainly did not affect his play. He hit .319 in 1940 and was one of the key reasons we ran away with the National League pennant.

Paul Derringer and Bucky Walters—the One-Two Punch

When the Cincinnati Reds won consecutive pennants in 1939 and 1940 our average time of game was about an hour and forty minutes. The reason we got our business done so efficiently? We fielded the best defense in the National League and had superlative pitching. In Paul Derringer and Bucky Walters we possessed the two finest hurlers in all of baseball. Both were no-nonsense guys who came to play, had great control, good fastballs, and a generous assortment of other stuff. They did not pace the mound, fix the cap, hitch the belt, mess with the resin bag, or shake off the catcher. Each stood on the mound, took the sign from Ernie Lombardi or whoever was catching, and threw the ball where it was intended to go. Each was baseball savvy and knew the strengths and weaknesses of each batter.

In 1939, Derringer won 25 and lost 7 with an earned run average of 2.93, while in 1940 he was 20-12, 3.06. Walters put up huge numbers as well, winning 27 and losing 11 in 1939 and posting a 22-10 record in 1940, with earned run averages of 2.29 and 2.48. In two years they won 94 games between them and finished what they began, collectively throwing 114 complete games out of 144 games started. They pitched until they won or lost and nobody ever counted the number of pitches they threw.

As alike as Bucky and Paul were on the mound, their personalities were quite different. Paul Derringer died on November 17, 1987 one month shy of his eighty-first birthday. Services were held at a small church in Osprey, Florida. The pastor gave a beautiful eulogy, testifying to Paul's devotion to family, his community service and his philanthropic good deeds. On my right in the church pew sat Gabe Paul, who was traveling secretary for the Reds during Derringer's best years in baseball. Gabe was later president of the Reds, the Indians, and the Yankees, and he knew Derringer better than anyone. Near the end of the eulogy he nudged me in the ribs and whispered in my ear, "Is he talking about Paul?"

After the services, Paul's wife, children, and grandchildren formed a

Paul Derringer and Bucky Walters after clinching the 1939 pennant.
They won 52 games between them that year.

receiving line and a better quality of people could not have been found. Somewhere between the time that I last saw him in 1942 and the time of his death forty-five years later, Derringer must have seen the light and been blessed with reformation. The guy with the Reds that I worked behind and liked had been a bit of a rogue.

My locker in the Reds' clubhouse always had a dozen or more new white inner stockings and woolen undershirts, courtesy of one Laird Jacobs. After my junior year at Duke, Laird had come over from Washington and Lee to play second base for Staunton in the semipro Virginia Valley League. We became good friends to my lasting benefit, because when Laird took over his daddy's cotton mill in Valdese, North Carolina, he saw to it that my supply of white inner stockings was constantly replenished. Derringer noticed that my supply of stockings was seemingly never-ending so he began to help himself to them, without asking. Some people might regard that as stealing, but since the guy was always pleasant and winning ball games, I thought it was in the team's interest to keep him happy. I simply acted like I never noticed. Then one day near the end of the season, Paul came into the clubhouse with a beautiful radio set built into a model sailing ship with sails flying from its masts and gave it to me. He said, "I've been using your inner socks all summer. This makes us square." I have no idea of the value of the radio and never asked. I do know that its value was far more than the cost of the stockings he might have purchased from Larry McManus, our clubhouse man.

Gabe Paul was a very important person to Derringer. A good traveling secretary like Gabe really knew the players, because he traveled with us on trains, ate with us on the road, reviewed our signed meal chits in the hotels, and satisfied our requests for seats in alien ballparks. He made himself available to do favors for the players and thereby promoted team morale. Paul Derringer was Gabe's best customer.

The pitcher was a convivial sort, was a big name in the game, and found company in most of the league's cities as we traveled. He loved good food and good whiskey and reciprocity required that he provide good seats for his friends at the Polo Grounds or Wrigley Field. At times he asked Gabe to leave two passes for "Joshua Knoblock," but the seats would be occupied by "Gertrude Ashley" and her sister. No matter, for the big guy was winning and the players had confidence with the ball in Paul's hand. To give the devil his due, he was smart enough to do his partying on the night after he pitched, and if he imbibed a bit of whiskey, he ran it out the next day chasing fungoes in the outfield.

It is a long time since I played ball with Paul Derringer, but if I was a manager and there was one big game to win, he is one of two men I would pick to pitch it. He knew what he was doing out there with a good fastball, great curve, and, I suspect, an occasional spitter. Paul relished combat, had the heart of a lion, and demonstrated a streak of meanness to hitters.

Bucky Walters, although entirely unlike Derringer, was equally as great a pitcher. Big, important games never fazed him, and he seemed to get better as the the game went on. We could count on him. He had a good fastball, a decent curve, and a sinker that bore in on righthanded batters. As a former infielder, he could field his position as well as anyone in the game. Best of all, he had good control and an excellent knowledge of the batters' weaknesses.

Pitchers are specialists, and not necessarily good athletes or good ballplayers. Bucky Walters came up with the Red Sox in the early 1930s as a third baseman. He could hit, he could lay down a sacrifice bunt, and he could hang a clothesline between third and first, so strong was his arm. After being converted to a pitcher by Jimmie Wilson of the woebegone Phillies, Walters toiled in Philadelphia for three years before Cincinnati's Warren Giles, looking for another starting pitcher, purchased him in June, 1938, for $50,000 cash and catcher Spud Davis and pitcher Al Hollingsworth. The results were immediate. Bucky went 11-6 for the Reds for the balance of 1938 before his remarkable 27 win year in 1939, which earned him the National League MVP award.

Bucky simply dominated in 1939 and 1940, leading the league both years in wins, in earned-run average, in innings pitched and in complete games. He also led the league in 1941 in innings and complete games.

Bucky was a quiet sort of fellow, not given to much conversation, but he was a fierce competitor. He could also be surprisingly sensitive. I remember his conversation in the subway about Dolph Camilli after a game against the Dodgers in Ebbets Field. Camilli, the Dodger first baseman, was a dangerous hitter with excellent power. Bucky had struck him out three times that afternoon. Dolph just could not lay off Walters' high inside fastball. "You know," he said, "I feel sorry for ole Dolph. He can't hit me." His expression of sadness was genuine.

I roomed with Bucky on the road during the 1940 season. We were in Boston in early August when Willard Hershberger, our backup catcher, tragically killed himself in the Copley Plaza Hotel, blaming himself for a ninth-inning loss two days earlier at the Polo Grounds. On this trip Walters was expecting his wife to join him in Boston, so he and I had separate rooms. Their son had developed an ear infection, however, and so his wife had to cancel her trip and stay in Cincinnati.

They had found Hershberger in his room after he failed to show up for a doubleheader at Braves Field. After dinner, Bucky came over to me in the lobby. He was very upset and said, "I want you to go up to your room and move all your stuff down to my room. I can't sleep by myself. I can't do it." I said, "Bucky, you'll be all right. All my stuff is unpacked in the bureau drawers and the bathroom and the closet and I'd have to pack it all. You'll be okay." So Bucky went off and I forgot all about my conversation with him until I went up to my room to go to bed a couple of hours later. I didn't have anything left in the room. Bucky had taken all my suits off the rack, all my toiletries and everything and moved them down to his room. He wanted no part of spending the night alone and was deeply affected by the tragedy.

Willard "Bill" Hershberger

The dog days of August are most trying for some ballclubs and many ballplayers. It is hot and humid and tempers are short, particularly in the pressure of a pennant race. August, 1940, killed Willard Hershberger.

Hershey was a young man of great character and a tough competitor. An excellent defensive catcher and fine hitter, he suffered the misfortune of coming up through the Yankee chain while Bill Dickey was catching, then finding himself behind Ernie Lombardi after he was sold to the Reds in 1938. Nevertheless, he made the most of limited playing opportunities, hitting .345 in 174 at-bats in 1939. In 1940 he hit .309 and, as manager McKechnie's number-one pinch hitter, collected a number of key hits. The Reds that year won 41 games by one run, and Hershey was responsible for a number of those wins. He never swung at a bad ball and struck out only sixteen times in 402 career at bats. You could send him up to bat in the dark of night and he would hit the ball somewhere.

Genetically, Hershey had an Achilles heel. He was a hypochondriac and asked Dr. Richard Rhode, the Reds trainer, to check him out almost every day. Perhaps he would ask Doc to look at his eyes to see if they weren't yellow. Rhode would assure Bill that his eyes were fine and had no yellow in them. The next day Hershey as back asking Doc to examine his tongue or ears, or some other part of his anatomy that he imagined was dysfunctional. We all respected and loved Hershey, but few if any of us realized that he had a problem. Some would go out of their way to tell him how bad he looked without realizing that they were adding to his problem. In late July, we were playing the Giants at the Polo Grounds. Lombardi had a badly sprained ankle and Hershey had been catching all the games, including some doubleheaders. Every day seemed hotter than the day before. McKechnie kept a small flask of brandy in Doc's medicine kit, and about the sixth or seventh inning of each game he would give Hershey a tablespoon of the stuff to bring some color back to his face. We were in a slump and had lost three games in a row. The worn-down Hershberger assumed the blame for each loss, lamenting, "If Lom was in there we wouldn't have lost."

On August 1, Bucky Walters was to pitch a night game against the Giants and we were hopeful of ending our slump. Sure enough, we entered the bottom of the ninth with a 4-1 lead, and with Bucky on the mound we were confident of victory. Walters began the inning, however, by walking Burgess Whitehead, and Mel Ott followed with a home run to make it 4-3. Then Bucky walked Mickey Witek, and Harry Danning hit another home run. A game that had been in the bag ended up in the loss column, 5-4. Hey, it happens, even to the best of teams.

In the Pullman leaving New York that night for Boston, Hershey sat on the side of his berth across the aisle from me blaming himself for the loss. "I called for the wrong pitches," he said. "If Lom had been in there, we wouldn't have lost. I've let the team down." I must have talked to him for an hour, reassuring him that it was not his fault and that it was not that important anyway. After all, we had about a ten-game lead. The next morning, August 2, we got up late and had breakfast together in the Copley Plaza Hotel. Hershey remained sick about the game, still blaming himself. Since we had an off day, I persuaded him to walk over to the Massachusetts Casualty Insurance Company with me. I was placing insurance business with them during the winter and I wanted to make a courtesy call while I was in town. After we were finished at the insurance company, I persuaded Bill to go with me to an afternoon movie, "Maryland, My Maryland" with Walter Brennan. The entire walk to the theater, he bewailed the miserable job he thought he was doing. He said, "Bill, it's all my fault. I've let the team down." I kept trying to boost him up, telling him, "You've done nothing of the sort." During the movie Hershey was antsy and got up and left several times, but always came back. After the movie, I was still trying to cheer him up as we walked back to the Copley Plaza. I never saw him again.

The next day we had a doubleheader with the Braves, and Hershey did not show up at the ballpark. It was not like him. He was a good competitor, a hustler, and a fighter with a lot of guts. Gabe Paul called the hotel manager and asked him to check Hershberger's room. Unfortunately, he was there. He had taken off all his clothes except his shorts, carefully surrounded the bathtub with newspapers so as not to make a mess, hacked at his throat with a safety razor until he hit his aorta, leaned over the tub, and bled to death. We were shocked and saddened and terribly depressed. Hershey was loved by everyone associated with the Reds. McKechnie pulled us together and we went on the win the pennant and the World Series against Detroit. We voted Hershey a full World Series share of $5,803.62 and sent the check to his mother in California.

Jimmie Wilson

Willard Hershberger's suicide created a catching crisis for the pennant-bound Reds. Lomabardi's bad ankle was not responding to treatment and it soon became apparent that he was not going to be able to catch in the World Series. Our third catcher, Bill Baker, was a rookie who had played very little and just did not have the necessary experience. But McKechnie came up with a master stroke. He drafted forty-year-old coach Jimmie Wilson to handle the position.

Wilson had come up with his hometown Philadelphia Phillies back in 1923 and quickly become a fine big league receiver. For fifteen years he played the position, including over five years with the famous Gashouse Gang in St. Louis. Back in Philadelphia, he managed the woeful Phillies from 1934 through the 1938 season, where he was responsible for switching Bucky Walters from third base to the pitcher's mound. In his first three years as manager he continued to catch most of the time. But he had caught only one game a year in 1938 and 1939, when he joined the Reds as a coach, and none at all in 1940. Only about three weeks remained in the 1940 season when McKecknie hatched his plan. He told Wilson, "You've got to get in there and get in shape."

So Jimmie began catching and his forty-year-old body suffered. Oh, how he suffered. We had a staff full of big strong-armed pitchers who could really throw hard. Derringer threw hard. Vander Meer threw hard. Junior Thompson, Jim Turner, Bucky Walters, Whitey Moore, Joe Beggs, Milt Shofner, Johnny Hutchings all threw hard. By the time the Series started, Wilson's catching hand had become red, swollen, and very sore. He had to soak his hand in hot water and Epsom salts every night just to be able to catch the next day, but he never complained.

About the time his hand got used to the pounding, he suffered charley horses in the back of both legs. I had a leg that was bothering me, too, and was going to the Netherland Plaza Hotel Health Club for treatment every day because I did not want the Reds or anyone else to know I was having trouble. There I ran into Wilson, getting diathermy and massages for his legs. At the ballpark Doc Rhode wrapped Jimmie's thighs in pads and adhesive tape before each game.

Jimmie caught six of the seven games in the World Series with those taped and aching legs and hit a cool .353. He also managed the only stolen base of the Series with those sore pins. A truly heroic performance by a man with the heart of a lion.

Wilson got the opportunity to manage again the following year. He managed the Cubs in 1941, 1942, and 1943. Jimmie successfully resisted any urge he might have had to put himself into a ballgame with the Cubs. He was fired in 1944, when the Cubs won only one of their first ten games. He died before his time on May 31, 1947. He was only forty-six years old.

Eddie Joost

Twenty-three-year-old Eddie Joost was another unlikely hero. Eddie had made the ballclub as a utility infielder out of spring training in 1939. He came from San Francisco, had played with the Missions in the old Pacific Coast League, and had had cups of coffee with Cincinnati in 1936 and 1937. In those years, Eddie was dour, not gregarious. Like me in a slightly different way, he seemed a little aloof and pretty much kept to himself. He was a determined young man, however, convinced of in his own ability. In 1939 and 1940, I think he felt he should be a regular infielder. He believed—as a good ballplayer should—he was better than Werber at third, Myers at short, or Frey at second. In 1939, he got into only 42 games. In 1940, however, he appeared in 88, including 78 at shortstop when Billy Myers was slumping or injured.

It's difficult to sit on the bench when you feel you're better than the men playing. What convinced me of the quality of the man was that he never complained and he never gave up on himself. Eddie shagged flies in the outfield, ran with the pitchers, and worked out in the infield so that he was ready whenever he had a chance to play. And when he played he was good.

In 1940, we breezed to the pennant, winning it by twelve games over the Dodgers. Just a few days before the World Series we received a staggering

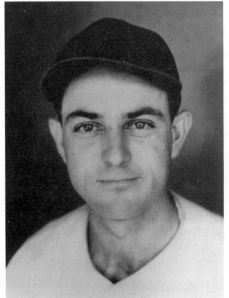

Willard Hershberger—
so tragic an end.

Jimmie Wilson—
a courageous catcher.

blow when Lonnie Frey tried to get a drink from the water cooler in the dugout. The iron lid slid off and crashed onto Lonnie's foot, breaking his toe and putting him out of the Series. Lonnie had played 150 games at second base for us that year and was one of our steadiest, most dependable performers. His loss was potentially devastating to our dreams of a world championship. Fortunately, Eddie Joost had kept himself fit to play. He stepped in and did a helluva job in the Series, playing errorless ball in the field and contributing several timely hits.

Eddie went on to have a fine major league career, later becoming a fixture at shortstop for the Athletics. He became one of the most popular players in Philadelphia because of his hustle and desire. He even managed the A's in 1954.

Billy Myers

Billy was our shortstop in 1939 and 1940, a fine fielder and pesky hitter with good speed afoot. He was one of the best-liked of all the Reds and had the sharpest needle. He was forever jabbing Lombardi, Derringer, or McCormick, but it was always apropos and never had any meanness behind it. Billy was a key to our success in those years. He was a little guy, five-foot-eight and about 160 pounds, and he seemed to wear down during the heat of the 1939 pennant race with the Cardinals. One day he came into the clubhouse before a doubleheader looking pale and drawn. He slumped down on his stool and said, "You guys better get some hits today," intimating that he was probably not going to get any himself. He was eating an apple and that was all the lunch he was going to have to last the doubleheader. He told us his wife wouldn't give him anything to eat because he refused to scrub the kitchen floor. Billy was married to a Pennsylvania Dutch woman half again as big as he was. Here was Billy, wearing down in the dog days of summer, fighting to bring a pennant to a city longing for success, and his wife demands that he scrub the kitchen floor before he leaves for a doubleheader. Billy played the two games with his usual steady fielding and chipped in a needed hit. The Reds whipped the Cardinals in the stretch and the good people of Cincinnati could finally put the Black Sox scandal behind them.

Fast forward to 1940. In late September, the Reds are well ahead in the pennant race, all cogs in the machine are working beautifully, and a second World Series check is assured. We are in St. Louis when Myers fails to show up at Sportsman's Park. A quick check reveals that he is not at the team hotel, either. He simply disappears, jumps the club.

The team quickly and quietly hires a detective who locates Myers in Columbus, Ohio. Myers tells general manager Warren Giles that he has personal problems and he is not coming back, even if he loses his World Series share. Giles finally talks Billy into rejoining the team for the Series against Detroit. The press is told that Myers has gone to Columbus on personal business with the club's permission. McKechnie's hair turns a shade whiter, but he has to play Myers in the Series. Joost, our only spare infielder, is playing second for the injured Frey. The only thing we can get out of Myers about his unscheduled absence is that he is worn out from too much abuse at home. The newspapers never uncover the true story, and Myers plays a steady shortstop during the Series, although he hits only .130. We win the Series in seven games, but McKechnie ages considerably, and after the season he trades Myers to the Cubs for outfielder Jim Gleeson. Billy hits only .222 in 24 games with the 1941 Cubs. It is his last year in the big leagues; at thirty-one he is finished as a ballplayer.

Lonny Frey

He was eighty-eight when I talked to him on the phone recently, has two new knees, and no longer bounces around on the balls of his feet as he did when he was a charter member of the Jungle Club. He has had quadruple bypass surgery, but his voice is strong and he laughs easily. Says he rides his bicycle daily for exercise, which he can do in Hayden, Idaho, without concern for traffic, and every evening at 7:30 he attends church. I tell him, "That's not going to get you into heaven."

He chuckles and says, "Probably not, but I'll give it a chance."

His oldest son Tom is an attorney in Hayden, and Lonny is surrounded by children, grandchildren, and great-grandchildren. His beloved wife Mary passed away some years ago, as did his first born, Jerry. Time has helped to ease the pain of these losses, and Mike, his youngest, lives nearby. Lonny seems at peace with the world.

Back up fifty-nine years and this same Lonny Frey is one of the principal reasons the Cincinnati Reds ended a twenty-year drought and won the 1939 pennant. He hit .291 and scored 95 runs in '39, followed by a .266 average for our World Championship team in 1940, while playing a mean second base. More than his statistics, however, were the intangible qualities Lonny brought to the team. Every club has players of outstanding talent and bad habits, but the team seldom wins without players of substance and character who come through when the chips are down. Lonny was one of those.

When I was sold to the Reds by Connie Mack in the late spring of 1939, I naturally began to assess my new teammates. You naturally form opinions from a ballplayer's perfomance on the field, but also from the way he dresses, the way he talks, and what he talks about. A newcomer observes these things and tends to gravitate toward the teammates with whom he feels most comfortable. A veteran like me tends to move slowly before settling into friendships, but Lonny Frey became my friend—after Dusty Cooke the best friend I had in thirteen years of professional baseball. Lonny was a veteran like me. He had come to the big leagues with Brooklyn in 1933 and played shortstop for the Dodgers for five years. After he spent 1937 with the Cubs, the Reds purchased him to plug a hole at second base, which he did with considerable skill and alacrity for seven years. By the time Lonny hung up his cleats in 1948 after late career stints with the Cubs, Giants, and Yankees, he had appeared in three All Star Games and three World Series.

Lonny and I shared many of the same habits and attitudes. He did not smoke or drink and was devoted to his wife Mary and his children, Jerry, Tom and Mike. He liked a movie after a ballgame and was a good sleeper. He was devoutly religious and a regular attendee at Catholic services on Sunday morning. I'm not Catholic, but I sometimes attended with him. Lonny could not explain to me the constant rising and sitting and rising at Mass or the Latin of the priests, but it did not matter. We both could have been doing worse. When we were playing at the Polo Grounds or Ebbets Field, Lonny loved to go to St. Patrick's Cathedral, burn a candle, put money in the poor box, and say a prayer. I went with him and made small contributions as well. If the next day I got the hits and he went for the collar, I'd tell him that Catholicism worked better for me than it did for him.

Lonny brought those intangible qualities of good humor and dependability to the ballpark every day. He had the stability and self-confidence gained from a secure family and spiritual life. He also had good physical assets as well. He was one of the fastest men on the Reds (he led the league with 22 stolen bases in 1940), and he used his speed to advantage both on offense and defense. Through it all "the Leopard" covered a great expanse of territory around second base and excelled at making the double play. He was steady. You could count on his doing the right thing at the right time during a game. I suspect that is still true.

Johnny "Double No Hit" Vander Meer

Johnny Vander Meer will always be remembered for pitching consecutive no-hitters, a feat that likely will never be duplicated and certainly never surpassed. He threw the first one on June 11, 1938, against Boston at Braves Field and the second four days later against the Dodgers in the first night game ever played at Ebbets Field. Vander Meer, a southpaw who stood six foot one, was only twenty-three years old when he hurled his twin masterpieces.

When I joined the Reds the following year I was surprised to learn that many of John's teammates were very cool toward him and harbored some resentment. They felt that he had made no effort to share the credit for his no-hit successes, even though a number of them had made outstanding defensive plays behind him in those games. But there was more to it than that. The Reds were headed for their first pennant in twenty years and John should have been a real asset to the club, but team morale sank considerably when he pitched. Here was a guy with a fastball to match Lefty Grove's and a curve ball far better than most, and his teammates did not want him on the mound. John was a hard worker, had good stamina, no bad habits, was goodlooking, friendly, and easy to talk to. What was the problem?

"Well," one player told me, "he'll get in a cab with you to ride to the ballpark and you have to pay the tab because all he has is a fifty-dollar bill. And he never reimburses you." Another volunteered an episode of paying for John's movie with no payback, and a third told me about buying him a milkshake with no reciprocity. Stories circulated about John borrowing

The author with the 1939 Reds.

money from rookies in spring training who could ill afford it, and never paying them back.

The feelings about John had little to to with baseball, but affected the way the team played behind him. I befriended John and tried to work out the problem. "Bill," he said to me, "I come from a poor family in Prospect Park, New Jersey. My father worked in a mill. There were times when I'd sit down to dinner and there was not enough food on the table. I made up my mind that if I ever got to the big leagues I was gonna keep every dollar I earned. It's just hard for me to turn lose of any money."

Although John had exceptional talent and should have been a star, he was plagued by wildness. Because of this and, perhaps, his teammates' attitude toward him, he went only 5-9 for our 1939 pennant winners. He showed little improvement in 1940. In late June, general manager Warren Giles sent this potential most valuable player back to the minors.

"Johnny," he advised, "I'm going to send you down to Indianapolis where you can take your regular turn. Jewel Ens is our manager there and he is going to work with you on your control and a few other things. You'll get the same salary as now; but John, when you ride in a cab, cover the fare. When you go to a movie, pay the way. I'll be checking with Jewel from time to time and if your progress is good I'll bring you back up."

John did make good progress, and Giles brought him back up in late August just as we were to play the rival Cardinals in a key series in the 1940 National League pennant race. Manager McKechnie decided to start Vander Meer in the first game before a packed house at Crosley Field. There was subdued grumbling among the Reds players: "What's McKechnie trying to do, lose the ballgame?"

And indeed, John proceeded to walk the first three Cardinal hitters— Don Gutteridge, Jimmy Brown, and Terry Moore. The Cardinals' heavy artillery came next in the persons of Johnny Mize, Ducky Medwick, and Enos "Country" Slaughter. All were hitting well above .300, had good power, and were clutch hitters. Why Bill McKechnie did not bring in a fresh pitcher remains puzzling, but he stayed the course. John tightened his belt, sucked in his gut, and blazed his fastball by all three, striking out as dangerous a trio as there was in the league. After that harrowing escape, John fairly breezed the rest of the game. Vander Meer, despite that key win, finished the season 3-1 in ten appearances. The team still harbored some resentment and voted not to give him any share of the World Series money. Commissioner Landis interceded and put him in for a half share.

John went on from his experience in 1940 to again become a good big league pitcher. Although he never fully conquered his wildness, he pitched for the Reds through 1949, with two years out for the war. In his best seasons he won 16, 18, 15, and 17 games for not-very-good teams. He retired as an active player in 1951 with 119 big league victories. In the early 1950s, I had lunch with Gabe Paul when he was in Washington, D.C., on business. We discussed a number of my old teammates and when we came to Vander Meer, he waxed enthusiastic, "John is managing our Savannah club and he is far and away the best manager we've got. He takes these young kids and gives them hours of patient instruction. If they are down on themselves or lonely, he takes them home to dinner. He's like an old mother hen with a brood of young chicks."

John died in 1997, during his eighty-second year. He had done well outside of baseball with a beer distributorship in Tampa. Not too long before he passed away we had lunch together and Gabe was there too, in a wheelchair. We laughed a lot, recalling many funny stories from fifty-seven years ago. Old John was still firing.

Ival Goodman—Ol' Mate
Ival was the right fielder during our two championship years in Cincinnati. Statistically, he did not put up big numbers, although in 1939 he hit .323, clubbing seven home runs and knocking in 84. I had the feeling then, and it remains with me, that he was a significant contributor to our successes.

His unique greeting at breakfast in the morning was, "Haiyah mate?" Or should you beat him to it, his response was, "Honolulu." He called everyone "Mate" though I doubt if he had ever been to Australia, and was called "Mate" by all in response. After dinner, he was an inveterate lobby-sitter, never given to controversy, taking in both sides of every argument, and making a contribution of merit now and again. Essentially a centrist. His speech wasn't elegant, but there was nothing wrong with his thinking, or his effort, or his display of guts on the ballfield.

Ival made the play of the year in our crucial late September series against St. Louis in 1939, sending the Cardinals home as second best. We lost two of the first three games, but could still clinch the pennant if we won the last one. With Paul Derringer struggling but keeping us in the game, the score was tied, 3-3, going into the seventh inning. Ducky Medwick led off with a screaming line shot over the head of center fielder Harry Craft, one of the better defensive outfielders in the game. Harry turned with the crack of the bat, ran back, and leaped for the ball, but it went over his outstretched glove and smacked off the center-field wall. Medwick raced around the bases with at least a triple in mind.

Ol' Mate in right field had a different idea. Following his instincts, he saw that the ball would exceed Craft's grasp and would likely carom past Harry off the wall. He raced over, grabbed the ball on the first bounce, and threw a perfect strike to me at third base. Medwick was out by twenty feet and the Cardinal rally died before it could begin. We went on to win the game and the pennant, 5-3, and the heart of a city was revived by one player's hustle and desire.

There was a time, however, when Mate's instincts failed him. It was a Sunday doubleheader in Crosley Field, and it was unusually hot and humid. McKechnie ordered the starters to skip batting and infield practice to conserve their energy. As I walked into the dugout, Matty Schwab, the groundskeeper, came in from third base with a thermometer in his hand. "Do you have any idea how hot it is out there?" he asked.

"No I don't, Matty, and I don't want to know."

Ignoring my request, he said, "Well this temperature gauge says that it is a hundred and ten."

Goodman and Harry Craft showed up with large cabbage leaves and put them on top of the ice in the dugout water cooler until game time. Then they put the leaves on top of their heads under their caps and took the field. They both had to leave the game in the the fifth or sixth inning because of nausea. We never did learn if there was a medical explanation for this phenomenon, but I decided not to try the cabbage leaf approach to the heat.

Gene Thompson

Junior. The guy had a full Christian name for sure, but when I first met him in spring training with the Cincinnati Reds in 1939 everyone called him Junior. He was only twenty-one, which I suppose accounts for it. I was 31, and delighted not to be called Senior.

Junior was a good-sized youngster at six-foot-one and 190 pounds and there was nothing junior about his stout right arm. He could throw hard and in most instances put it where he wanted it. There was also nothing junior about his commitment to the game or his will to win. He had great poise for a twenty-one-year-old. In pressure situations he could be best described as unflappable.

It was probably no accident that his arrival coincided with two consecutive pennants. That first year all he did was win 13 while losing only five as a spot starter and reliever. His earned run average was a sparkling 2.54 and he would undoubtedly have won Rookie of the Year honors if there had been such an award back then. He followed that sparkling performance with a 16-9 record in the world championship year of 1940 with 17 complete games in 31 starts. When the World Series against the Tigers rolled around, Junior sat out the first four games. McKechnie started aces Derringer and Walters in Games 1 and 2. Jim Turner got the call for Game

3 (he had gone 14-7 with a 2.89 era), and then Derringer came back for Game 4, since he had been knocked out of the box in the second inning of the first game.

Game 5 was played in Detroit and, since the Series was tied two games each, it was a pivotal contest. McKechnie decided to start Thompson, but he wanted to spare Junior as much pressure as possible and let him get a good rest. So he didn't tell Gene or announce his starting pitcher until just before game time. Junior had married a lovely young lady, Dorothy, in 1939 and she was seated in the box seats with the other wives. She had not imagined in her wildest dreams that Junior would be called upon to pitch in enemy territory, or anywhere else, on such a pressure-packed occasion. When the announcer bawled over the stadium amplifying system, "Pitching for the Reds, Junior Thompson," it was more than Dorothy could take. She gasped, "Oh, my God" and passed out in her seat.

It was a precursor of things to come. Gene did not have one of his better

Ival "Ol' Mate" Goodman—
a fine man in the clutch.

Gene "Junior" Thompson—
unflappable under pressure.

days and lost, 8-0, to Bobo Newsom, who pitched a three-hitter only a few days after his father died from a heart attack the morning following the first game. Junior's outing turned out not to matter, since we beat Detroit two straight back in Cincinnati to win the Series four games to three.

Injuries unhappily took their toll on Junior, the war intervened, and he was called up to serve, before finishing his career with the New York Giants in 1946 and 1947. A finer baseball man never lived, however, and at age eighty-two Gene is still scouting for the San Diego Padres and living happily with Dorothy in Arizona.

Junior, like many ballplayers of my era, liked to hunt and fish in the off-season. While we were teammates we often read magazines such as *Field and Stream*, *Sports Afield*, and *Ducks Unlimited* during the long train rides and talked of traveling to faraway places after the season to go bird hunting. During the 1942 season, I read in *American Field* of a place called Buffalo Lodge on a large lake in Manitoba. The story described the sky there as black with ducks. Although I was then with the Giants, I wrote Junior and Doc to ask if they cared to indulge their fantasies after the season and they did. In the fall, Junior, Doc Rhode (it seems that every trainer in those days was called Doc—Doc Painter with the Yankees, Doc Wood with the Red Sox, Doc Ebling with the A's, and Doc Rhode with the Reds) and I joined forces in Moose Jaw, Saskatchewan to lay waste to an overabundance of duck, pinnated grouse, and Hungarian partridge.

It did not turn out as we planned, however, and we never did see Buffalo Lodge. We ended up with a guide named Art Getson, who, when not shepherding hunters from the States over miles of stubble fields, was an engineer driving a locomotive. The guy was amiable, knew the territory, and had a nose for game like a bird dog for quail. Each day we hunted with Art we bagged our limit of duck, grouse, and partridge; possibly more than our limit.

Since we were hunting three kinds of game, we carried in separate pockets three different numbers of shot: #4 for ducks, #8 for grouse, and

#10 for partridge. When we returned to Getson's automobile to change hunting locations, Junior would invariably shuck out the shells from his pump shotgun while inside the car. I told him I thought this was danger-ous, and so did Doc. Junior's response was always, "Aw, I've got the safe on. There's no danger. I do this all the time."

On our last day out of Moose Jaw we shot ducks, and then prepared to leave in the late afternoon. Getson was behind the wheel ready to go. Junior was in the back seat pumping out shells. Doc Rhode and I were standing outside, doing the same, when *Baroom*! The shot from Junior's gun blew a hole in the top of Art's car about as big as a frying pan. Ever the stoic, Art did not even turn around. Sadly he shook his head, mumbling, "I knowed it, I knowed it all along. I knowed he was gonna do it." It cost Gene something like $100 to get the hole repaired and replace the lining. I suppose Doc was circumspect and kept the misadventure to himself. I was, retired and out of the circle, so I felt no such contraints.

Al Simmons

Al Simmons was one of the great hitters of his day, and had the swag-ger to prove it. Dubbed "Bucketfoot Al" by the press because of his habit of striding away from the plate with his left leg as he swung, he compiled a lifetime batting average of .334 in twenty big league seasons. In 1929, 1930, and 1931, when Connie Mack's Athletics won consecutive pennants by large margins, Simmons hit .365, .381, and .390. Posting those kinds of numbers, it may be easy to forget that you were born Aloys Szymanski. Al did forget. He walked with a strut and had little to do with mere mortals who hit in the .280s or .290s. To put it plainly, he had a swelled head.

Al was one of the better-paid Athletics, probably ahead of Foxx, Cochrane, Grove, or Earnshaw. What he earned he kept. He was penurious with clubhouse attendants both on the road and at home. Clubhouse boys, then and now, provide a great many services to ballplayers. They take care of uniforms and equipment, and they run errands. Most ballplayers are generous with tips for these young men. Al wasn't. He also carryed his own bag from the Pullman car to the taxicab to avoid tipping a redcap. He did the same at the hotel to avoid paying a bellhop. He didn't spend much on himself, either. His A's teammates could never understand why he chose to rent a room in a home beyond the right-field wall of Shibe Park in the full glare of the western sun.

The days of glory, of course, eventually end for one and all. Reflexes dull, legs get heavier, eyes fail. Behavior patterns usually change as well. On a ballclub folks once ignored are now solicited to go to a movie. That advice Herb Pennock gave me when I first joined the Yankees in 1930—"Be nice to everyone on your way up because you're going to meet a lot of them on the way back down."— comes into play.

At least Al Simmons was a nice guy on the way down. He was purchased by the Reds from the Red Sox late in the 1939 season. He appeared in only nine regular season games for us, with three hits in 21 at bats. He started one game in the World Series against the Yankees and cracked a double in four tries. Throughout his brief time with the Reds, he was a friendly and agreeable chap at the ballpark, on the train, and in the dining room. On his way down he was a positive influence on our ballclub, even though his contributions on the field were inconsequential. The Reds released Simmons after the 1939 season and he hung on through most of the war as a player-coach back with the Athletics. He was deservedly elected to the Hall of Fame in 1953 before passing away just past his fifty-fourth birthday in 1954.

A good many other ballplayers contributed to our success in 1939 and 1940, fellows like Harry Craft, Jim Turner, Wally Berger, Whitey Moore, Mike McCormick, Morrie Arnovich, Lee Grissom, Frenchy Bordagaray, Joe Beggs, Lew Riggs, and Les Gamble.

A few more had a cup of coffee or two with us in those years, guys like Mike Dejan, Wes Livengood, Vince DiMaggio, Johnny Rizzo, Nino

Taking a cut at Crosley Field.

Bongiovanni, Les Scarsella, Johnny Niggeling, Jim Weaver, Jimmy Ripple, Peaches Davis, Johnny Hutchings, Bill Baker, Hank Johnson, Pete Naktenis, Milt Shofner, Dick West, Milt Galatzer, and Art Jacobs. Future Yankee third baseman, cardiologist, and American League president Bobby Brown even worked out with us for a couple of weeks in 1940 as a sixteen-year-old high schooler. He had a great batting stroke even then.

Those Reds ballclubs were great teams, with the emphasis on team. We had character and talent and the mangerial wisdom of Bill McKechnie. We are all largely forgotten now, even the stars like McCormick, Walters, and Derringer. Until Ernie Lombardi made it in 1986, the '39 and '40 Reds were the only repeat pennant winners in history without a player in the Hall of Fame. It is a shame that Derringer and Walters still are not in the Hall.

I remember them all fondly. Oh, what a time we had!

17 COLLATERAL BENEFITS

There are always collateral benefits to being a ballplayer. Your name is in the box score every day and once in a while you make the headlines of the sports page. Half of our games were on the road, so much of our time was spent in hotels. It was not unusual after breakfast to buy a morning newspaper, find a comfortable chair under a good light in the lobby, and read about the heroics of the day before, or to learn if the official scorer gave you an error on the ground ball that hit a pebble and bounced over your glove. Sometimes a fellow traveler, always a male, would recognize your youthful, tanned countenance, take an adjoining chair, and attempt to engage you in conversation. The ballplayer, more likely than not, would soon get up, proceed to the elevator, and flee to the privacy of his room. A few would continue to sit, fold up the morning paper, and give the fan the time of day. After dinner, the routine changed a bit, depending on the heat of the day, whether you had won or lost, and whether you had played one game or two. If you had won a doubleheader, you might feel quite satisfied, sip a cold beer and enjoy a leisurely dinner with teammates. After dinner you sat in the lobby and thought about the money you were getting for all the fun you were having playing ball. If you had lost, conversation was limited, and you were likely to hop a cab and head for a movie to forget about the problems of the day.

When I was with the Reds, we stayed at the beautiful Copley Plaza Hotel in Boston when we played the Bees. The dining room was elegant, with food to match. The place was so nice that the players rarely left the hotel after dinner, content to sit in small groups in the comfort of the lobby. The Bees were a generally a pushover in those days, so we often had the victory of the day to savor.

Sometimes when the horses were running at Suffolk downs we were joined by Samuel D. Riddle, owner of Man O' War, probably the greatest racehorse of all time. Mr. Riddle also owned the Rumford Baking Powder Company and two large horse farms, one near Berlin, Maryland, and the other out of Lexington, Kentucky, but it was as a knowledgeable baseball fan that I came to know him. He was rotund, about sixty-five years of age, snow-white thinning hair on top, and a neatly trimmed gray pencil mustache. He was a bachelor, soft spoken, with a pleasant demeanor. Ballplayers pressed him for tips on his horses. "No, I cannot help you," was his inevitable response. "I don't know when they will win. My trainers don't know when they will win."

"Don't you bet on your horses, Mr. Riddle?"

"Oh, on occasion I might bet $2 on a race, but nothing more than that."

Ballplayers who bet on the races, in my experience, were few. Judge Landis, the commissioner, frowned on it. Those who did were driving modest cars. Mr. Riddle came to Boston in a chauffeured Rolls Royce.

In January 1942, the Reds sold me up the river to the Giants. (Up the river is apt, because the Giants finished third in '42—one rank ahead of the Reds.) The Giants trained in Belair, Florida, a bit out of Miami, and they housed us at the Bellevue Biltmore, a very large and plush resort hotel. One morning after breakfast, as I walked to the elevator to go up to my room I saw a former classmate of mine at Duke. I had known him well enough to roll up my morning newspaper, stick it in his back and tell him, "Stick 'em up." He turned slowly, and after an exchange of pleasantries, he said softly, "You damn fool. I could've killed you." He was in the Secret Service, a bodyguard to Cordell Hull, the Secretary of State, who was in the Tower Suite. He showed me the automatic inside his coat. I did not think it necessary to ask how quick he was on the draw.

About a week later, I saw my old classmate again and he asked if I would do Mr. Hull a courtesy and visit him in his suite. He had told the Secretary about our meeting and our friendship at Duke and was surprised to find that he read the sports pages and was a knowledgeable fan. He particularly wanted to ask me how, as reported in a Shirley Povich column in the Washington *Post*, I was able to sell a life-insurance policy to a player sliding into third base. Mr. Hull greeted me cordially. He laughed and smiled a lot. "Tell me how you managed that life insurance sale on a man sliding into third," he asked. I had to explain that it did not happen that way. One day after infield practice, before an exhibition game in Orlando, while I was playing for the Reds, I went into the Washington Senators' clubhouse to change my wet undershirt. Sitting on a stool in front of his locker, examining some papers, was my good friend and former teammate, Rick Ferrell. The papers were an insurance proposal and Rick asked me to come over and explain a few things to him. At that moment Arch McDonald, the radio voice of the Senators, came in and asked, "What are you old Red Sox buddies visiting about?"

"Arch, I'm reviewing an insurance presentation," Rick replied.

In the press box during the game McDonald told the story to Povich who thought it good enough to embellish upon it in his column. It got me a meeting with the Secretary of State.

In the summer of 1942, the world was at war. President Roosevelt had ruled that baseball should continue as a needed recreational diversion and morale booster, and I was playing third base for the Giants. When we played the Dodgers in Ebbets Field, our route by cab or car took us by the docks. There rested the British luxury liner Queen Elizabeth, now painted black and festooned fore, aft, and midships with all varieties of guns. On the wharf, waiting to be loaded, were acres of tanks, armored vehicles, trucks, cannon, and medical vehicles. The next day the wharfs were cleared and the Queen Elizabeth gone, well out into the Atlantic on the way to England.

New York City was surrounded by enormous bases training armed forces personnel, many of whom would land on Omaha or Utah beach as part of the Normandy invasion. An efficient United Service Organization recruited entertainers from show business and the world of sports to provide entertainment for the thousands of troops at the large amphitheaters set up on the bases.

The USO called Horace Stoneham, the owner of the Giants, and asked if he would designate a player to visit on a specified night, to speak and answer questions from the audience. My turn came one Sunday evening. A car picked me up, and we cruised to Jack Dempsey's Restaurant, where the Manassa Mauler joined me. I was surprised, to say the least. Dempsey was a friendly, well-mannered, well-groomed guy with no visible scars from his bouts. He was the old shoe type, without affectation. We had an hour to ride and he did all of the talking. His high-pitched voice was in marked contrast to his rugged appearance. I learned he did not own or even have money in "his" famous restaurant. He was paid extremely well to lend his name and to meet and greet during the dinner hour. He sat and visited for a moment with customers and ask if their steaks were to their liking. This usually posed no hardship, he said, because he liked people and people seemed to enjoy his company. Once in a while, there were problems. "On occasion," he told me, "some young fellow will come into the restaurant with a couple of broads, and after a few drinks he'll say, 'There's Dempsey over there—never had no guts—never could fight,' and come over and slap my face."

"I can't believe it," I said. "What do you do?"

"I have to leave the table, run into my office, and lock the door. You see," he explained, showing his great, formidable hands, "my fists are considered lethal weapons and if I hit the guy it might kill him. All the good will would be gone and I'd have no job."

I asked if he was married or had children. "No," he responded. "Was married to a lesser movie star, but it didn't work out. We're now divorced. Hired a detective to monitor her activities and he called one evening to have me meet him at one of the local hotels. She was on a date in room 1020 and he had a key. We walked in and there they were. He says, 'Can you identify her?'

"'Yeah,' I said. 'I'd know that ass anywhere.'"

"How about the Tunney fights?" I asked.

"Gene Tunney and I are good friends. He is an intelligent man and was a damn good fighter. I thought I won the long-count fight. The second fight was a point decision, but those fights are long past. Let dead dogs lie."

Some years later I was returning from a hunting trip and ran into Dempsey in the Chicago airport. He remembered with pleasure our evening entertaining the servicemen. I feel fortunate that baseball allowed me the opportunity to visit with one of the great fighters of the century.

18 SHIRLEY POVICH AND GABE PAUL: LEGENDS OFF THE FIELD

Not all the good people I knew during my time in baseball were ballplayers. Baseball writers, executives, and clubhouse boys were all an integral part of major league baseball and I enjoyed friendships with many. Two with whom I formed lifetime friendships were Shirley Povich and Gabe Paul.

We lost one of the finest journalists of the twentieth century in June, 1998, when Shirley Povich passed away at the age of ninety-two. One of the true legends among sportswriters, Shirley had written for the Washington *Post* for some seventy-five years. Observing and writing is what he did, and he did it well. Indeed, he wrote his last column the day before he died.

Shirley grew up in Bar Harbor, Maine, in the only Orthodox Jewish family in town. He arrived in Washington as a seventeen-year-old undergraduate at Georgetown University, a protege of *Post* publisher Ned McLean, for whom he had caddied in Bar Harbor. His first day in Washington, he traveled to McLean's private golf course, where he met and caddied for Warren G. Harding, the president of the United States. Povich never left the nation's capital, joining the *Post*'s sports department in 1924 and becoming, by 1926, the youngest sports editor in the country. He was twenty-one.

Indeed, it was the winter of 1926 when our paths first crossed in rather unusual circumstances. It was my senior year at McKinley Tech High School and we were playing Eastern High for the District of Columbia prep basketball championship at the George Washington University gymnasium. Povich was the official timekeeper. In those days, the timekeeper fired a gun loaded with blanks at the end of each period. At the end of the game, Tech was one point ahead when time expired. Shirley lifted his gun when his timepiece indicated no time left, and tried to fire. But the gun would not go off, and the game went on. In desperation, the resourceful Povich worked his way through the screaming crowd to one of the bands, grabbed the cymbals and hurled them onto the middle of the floor to get everyone's attention and stop the game. In the interim, both Eastern and Tech had raced up and down the floor, shot at the basket and missed. Thus, Tech hung on to its one point "overtime" victory.

Shirley was kind to me from the start, selecting me for his all-star five in basketball and later that spring at shortstop on his all-star prep baseball nine. At that age it was tremendously exciting for me to see my name and photograph in the paper. When I went off to Duke that fall and busied myself playing basketball and baseball, he included a favorable blurb about me in the *Post* from time to time. My parents, who were living in Berwyn, Maryland, now part of College Park, clipped the blurbs and sent them down to me at school.

Later, when I played in the American League and my team visited Griffith Stadium to play the Senators, Shirley would sometimes slip into the visitors dugout before the game for a quote or, he hoped, a scoop. I genuinely liked Shirley and was glad that he seemed to like me, because a sour pen in the hands of a literate sportswriter can be devastating, as he proved in his long feud with Washington Redskins' owner George Marshall.

Marshall brought the Redskins to Washington in 1937, after several seasons in Boston. He refused to sign black players through the 1950s, and Povich called him on it for years, once writing that "Jim Brown, born ineligible to play for the Redskins, integrated their end zone three times yesterday." In another column he wrote that "the Redskins colors are burgundy, gold, and Caucasian."

When the Reds opened the 1939 World Series against the Yankees in

New York, Shirley called from the lobby of our hotel before Game 1 and asked if he could come up for a visit. He got his own private scoop on the outcome of the Series from geniuses Frey and Werber, who predicted a Reds' victory based on the superior pitching of Derringer and Walters. I never did see what Povich wrote, but it's just as well. The Yankees beat us four straight.

The next time I saw Shirley was just before we were to play the seventh game of the 1940 World Series against the Tigers. He plopped down beside me in the dugout and said, "Bill, did you know that if you get two hits today you'll set a new record for most hits in a Series?"

"No," I said, "I didn't know that but put them down in your book."

Leading off the game against Bobo Newsom, I hit a line drive that Hank Greenberg picked off the left field wall, and that was my best effort of the day. My failure to live up to my bravado meant nothing, however, for we won that seventh game by a 2-1 squeaker and were world champions. After the Series, Shirley came out to Berwyn with his cameraman, took photos of my mother and grandmother and wrote a nice story on "country boy makes good."

We stayed in touch after I retired from baseball, and in 1955 Shirley called me at my offices at the National Press Building in Washington. He wanted to write a story about my son, Bill, who had been an All-American first baseman at Duke in 1952 and 1953, but had turned down the overtures of major league baseball to study for an MBA from the University of Pennsylvania's Wharton School of Business. Shirley found it difficult to understand how a young man with obvious talent could turn down an $85,000 bonus to go back to school, but he wrote a kindly piece anyway.

My last contact with Shirley was occasioned by his eulogy in the *Post* of Monte Weaver. Monte had been a fine pitcher for the Senators, breaking in with a phenomenal 22-10 record in 1932 and following that with a 10-5 record for the pennant-winning 1933 team. I had known Monte since the summer of 1927 when he pitched for Valdese in the semipro Western

Carolina League where I played shortstop for Newton in the same league. Weaver was not only a fine pitcher, but, of greater moment, he was a true gentleman and scholar, holding a master's degree in mathematics. When his arm wore out he earned a living teaching math for many years at Emory & Henry College in Virginia.

Povich penned a beautiful piece about Monte when he died and I was moved to write and compliment him. I added that I hoped I would die before he did so that he could do a piece about me. Shirley was equally gracious in his response and suggested that I would fare equally well because "you did so many things well." Since Shirley passed away and I'm still around, I guess it's me writing a eulogy for him. He was truly one of the good ones.

Gabe Paul passed away on April 26, 1998, at the age of eighty-eight. He is most remembered as an astute baseball executive, directing the fortunes of four major league teams during his career. Perhaps his crowning achievement was rebuilding the New York Yankees into world champions during the late 1970's.

I got to know Gabe when he was traveling secretary of the Reds. He was from Rochester, New York, and got his start in baseball in 1920 at the age of ten when he served as batboy for the hometown Red Wings of the International League. George Stallings, who had managed the Miracle Braves to the 1914 National League pennant, was the manager, and enlisted young Gabe to give the home team an edge. When the Red Wings were ahead in the late innings, Gabe claimed that Stallings sent him to a grocery store behind left field, where he had balls stored in an ice box. The balls, deadened by the cold, would be slipped into the umpire's supply of balls for the visitors' final at-bats.

At eighteen, he was hired by a local paper as a part-time sportswriter for $1.50 a week. Shortly thereafter Warren Giles, the newly named president of the Red Wings, hired him for six weeks to accompany the team to

*Gabe Paul—from traveling secretary par excellance
to two-time Baseball Executive of the Year.*

its Louisiana spring training site and file stories to the Rochester papers. He ended up working for Giles for twenty-three years. Giles named him traveling secretary of the Red Wings in 1934 and when Giles became general manager of the Reds in 1936 he brought Gabe along to do the same job.

I played on five ballclubs over a thirteen-year period and Gabe Paul was the only traveling secretary I encountered who truly believed that the players came first, that keeping them happy resulted in better on-field performance, more profit for the ownership, and higher degree of civic pride. It is the little things that make the difference.

With twenty-four players on a ball club with different temperaments, educational backgrounds, and attitudes, it takes a highly skilled ringmaster to keep them all content, and Gabe had that talent. When you arrived in Tampa for spring training, he gave you a schedule of all exhibition games on the way north, the hotels at which the team would be staying, what cabs to take from the train to the hotel and whether they were prepaid or player-paid to be reimbursed. The where, what, when, and why were all spelled out for the players, to their pleasure.

At times during the regular season, more often than not on days with sellout crowds, friends or relatives of players would call and say they were in town and would like tickets for the game. Was Gabe hard to find? Did he snarl at you and say, "You know damn well we're sold out. I've got no tickets." No, to the contrary, Gabe was always available and helpful. "What is his name? I'll see that he is seated. If necessary, I'll put chairs in the aisle."

Such affability creates good will, and the ballplayer is appreciative and plays a little harder. Attention to detail counts, too. In the dog days of summer, having a traveling secretary who leaves nothing to chance can help keep the club's morale high. For example, on train trips, Gabe always made sure that there were enough steaks to go around, large and tender. He made sure that the railroad knew that the Reds spent a lot of money transporting their athletes and that they should be treated right. Everyone got an assigned lower berth, with Lombardi put back with the newspaper-men because of his loud snoring. Gabe thought of everything for our comfort and convenience.

By being so aware of the little things that count, Gabe went on to an exemplary career in baseball. When Warren Giles was named National League president in 1951, Gabe became the Reds' general manager and stayed with them through 1960, building the team that won the 1961 National League pennant. With the Reds in 1957, he hatched a scheme even more enterprising than the old frozen baseballs stunt. At the time, fans voted for the starting members of the All Star team by checking names on ballots printed in newspapers. Gabe arranged for the two Cincinnati papers to print the Reds' starting lineup every day in a "sample" ballot which indicated where the fans could mark their "X." He had similar ballots distributed at Crosley Field. The one exception to a Reds player on the ballot was at first base, where Paul magnanimously listed Stan Musial of the Cardinals instead of George Crowe, since the game was to be played in St. Louis.

The Reds were on their way to a fourth-place finish, but when the All Star ballots were tabulated Reds players were named to seven of the eight starting positions, including the entire outfield (Frank Robinson, Gus Bell, and Wally Post), the catcher (Ed Bailey) and three-quarters of the infield (Johnny Temple, Roy McMillan, and Don Hoak). Commissioner Ford Frick responded to the understandable outrage and unilaterally removed Bell and Post as starters, replacing them with a couple of runners-up named Mays and Aaron. The scam also resulted in the vote being taken away from the fans until 1970.

After a brief stint with the fledgling Houston franchise, Gabe became general manager of the Cleveland Indians, where he served for eleven years. In 1973, he was lured away by new Yankee owner George Steinbrenner. He stayed for five turbulent years, during which the Yankees won two pennants and a world championship, before rejoining the

Indians' organization as president until his retirement in 1984. Along the way he was twice named major league Executive of the Year.

Gabe and Shirley were special people who spent their lives, not on a ballfield, but in and around baseball. They were lifelong friends, and although they had long and fruitful lives, I miss them both.

19 SALARY WARS

No one had yet conceived of the idea of agents in the 1930s. The reserve clause was alive and well, and salary negotiations took place between owner and player on an annual basis. If they could not agree on a figure, the player did not play, period. Despite the reserve clause, I managed to gain some leverage in salary negotiations because I had an education and something I could do away from baseball. But that gets ahead of the story. My first real salary dispute occurred in the spring of 1936. Boston Red Sox owner Tom Yawkey offered me a contract for about $2,000 less than I thought I merited. I grumbled to Mr. Yawkey, but signed the contract and began the season in a less-than-happy frame of mind. Having signed to play, however, I intended to put forth my best effort everyday. Early in the season, we were playing the Yankees in Fenway Park when one of the New York hitters lofted an exceedingly high pop foul in my general direction at third. A brisk wind carried the ball toward the visitor's dugout with me in hot pursuit. With eyes glued to the ball, I missed the first step in the Yankee dugout and fell over the other two, ending up flat on my back. The Yankees were, of course, no help at all and were in fact calling me some vulgar names. The ball, meanwhile, just missed the concrete roof of the dugout and somehow found its way into my outstretched glove.

In the locker room after the game, Johnny Orlando, our clubhouse boy, told me that Mr. Yawkey would like to see me for a few minutes. I went up to his office after showering and dressing and he greeted me with a handshake and asked me to sit down. "Bill," he said, "you were unhappy about your contract this spring but you have never lost hustle. That catch you made today in the Yankee dugout was without a doubt the greatest I've ever seen. It was worth $2,000 to me and I'm going to put it into your contract." It was a pleasure to play for the likes of Thomas Austin Yawkey.

I suppose I had become more interested in the financial rewards of baseball because of the conversation I've already described in the winter of 1935 with orthopedic surgeon Dr. George Bennett at Johns Hopkins University hospital in Baltimore. It followed that long season of playing third base for the Red Sox on the big toe I had injured in 1934 trying to kick the water bucket a la Lefty Grove. The toe was so painful that I had to favor it continually and that began to create problems in the backs of both thighs. Doc Logan, the Red Sox trainer, carried a diathermy machine on all road trips to apply heat to the toe before each game and he regularly massaged my legs. So, 1935 was a less than enjoyable season and I was not very happy with myself. I had a wife and children, ages four and one, to support and a mortgage on a nice home to pay, and my cussedness had created a future earnings problem of real moment. The end of my baseball career loomed with the resultant loss of a nice income. I was twenty-seven years old.

I had the surgery Dr. Bennett recommended, massaged the toe gently with olive oil as he prescribed, and managed to stay in the big leagues for seven more seasons. But I was always in pain, and I never knew when that right toe would act up and make it impossible for me to perform up to professional standards.

So each fall, as soon as the season was over, I reported to my father's business, the Werber Insurance Agency, and studied about and sold life, health, and accident insurance. It was a humbling experience, but each year I increased my knowledge and earnings and prepared for the time when I could no longer play baseball.

When I was traded by the Red Sox to the Philadelphia Athletics after the 1936 season, Lefty Grove had a parting admonition for me. Then with the Red Sox, he had pitched nine years for Connie Mack in Philadelphia. He told me, "Don't let the old gentleman ever get you up into his cupola office. If you do, you're gonna want to pay him to let you play for the A's."

I had a good year for the A's in 1937, hitting close to .300 and tying Ben Chapman for the league lead in stolen bases with 35. I hoped for a nice raise, and accepted a modest one without quibbling. I did vow to do better the next year, however. Thus, after the 1938 season with the Athletics I was emboldened to ask Connie Mack for a raise of $1,500. My timing may not have been great, since we finished in the basement, 46 games out of first place, with a record of 53-99. Nonetheless, I made my request by mail and, mindful of Grove's advice, declined Mr. Mack's invitation to come to Philadelphia to talk about my contract. He later called to suggest a meeting when he was in Washington to visit his old friend Clark Griffith, but I pleaded a prior commitment.

Finally, after I had dodged him for several months, Mr. Mack wrote me a long letter in January, 1939. In it he explained that the 1938 season had been poor at the gate, that he didn't expect things to get better, and that the 1939 payroll was already expected to produce a deficit. He also mentioned disappointment in my 1938 performance and concluded by telling me that the contract I was about to get in the mail would contain the top figure he would offer me. The contract came without the $1,500 raise, prompting me to reply impetuously that I knew he had had a bad year, I knew his payroll was too high, and I knew he was going to have another bad year coming up. Then I impudently advised him to sell the ballclub and get into a more profitable line of business. One does some foolish things in life, and I did a foolish thing by responding to Mr. Mack in that manner.

I heard nothing more from Mr. Mack until early April, when spring training was almost over. By now I was doing pretty well in my father's insurance business, and I did not have to play baseball to earn a living. I still wanted to play ball, however, so I worked out with the University of

Maryland baseball team because their coach, Burton (Ship) Shipley, was a good friend.

In a late March practice game between the varsity and scrub team, I played third base for the scrubs. The varsity was resplendent in new black, gold, and gray uniforms while I was attired without a cap in khaki pants and a gray sweatshirt. Despite my appearance, I had a pretty fair day, knocking a couple of home runs, stretching a single into a double, and fielding third flawlessly. The next day the Washington *Post* questioned Ship's judgment in not issuing a varsity uniform to the third baseman on the scrub team.

During dinner one evening soon afterward, I got a phone call from Bill Hottel, an old friend and a Washington *Star* reporter. He told me, "It just came over the AP wire that you've been sold to Cincinnati. Are you going to report?"

I said, "I don't know. I haven't heard from Cincinnati. This is the first I've heard of it at all."

After nine years in the American League, I thought it might be interesting to play in the National League. A little later that evening the phone rang again. It was Warren Giles, the general manager of the Reds. "Bill," he said, "we have purchased your contract from the Athletics and we would like you to report to camp in Tampa as soon as possible."

"Mr. Giles," I replied, "there is a difference of $1,500 between what Mr. Mack offered me and what I want to play ball." Giles said, "I'm sorry. We can't pay as much money as they do in the American League." So I said, "Well, then I won't be there." "I guess I'll just have to return you to the Athletics then," he said.

About an hour later the phone rang once again. It was Mr. Mack calling from the A's training camp in Lake Charles, Louisiana. "Bill, why won't you report to Cincinnati?" he asked. "They won't pay me any more than you offered, sir," I explained, "and I won't play for that." He said, "I'll tell you what I'll do. You go on and report to Cincinnati and I'll pay you $1,500 out of the purchase price." He was getting about \$12,500 from the Reds for my contract. "No, I don't want your \$1,500," I responded. "I want it in a contract as part of my regular pay with Cincinnati." "In that case," Mr. Mack said with irritation, "Just make a deal for yourself with any club."

I did not like that idea either, because any other team would ultimately have to deal with Mr. Mack to get my services, so I said, "No, Mr. Mack, you own my contract. You make the deal." "I'm sorry, then, Bill," Mr. Mack said. "Good night." He hung up.

A little while latter the phone rang again. Mr. Giles was on the line. "Why don't you fly down to Tampa and talk about it? We will pay for your plane fare." "Mr. Giles," I said, "There isn't anything to talk about. Put \$1,500 more in my contract and I'll be there." "Are you in shape to play?" he asked. "I'm in good shape, been working out with the University of Maryland." He said, "Well, I don't know. I'll have to talk to Bill McKechnie, and he isn't back from an exhibition game in Miami."

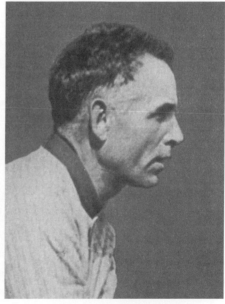

Tom Yawkey—
a pleasure to play for.

Clark Griffith—generosity
without fanfare.

After every phone call my wife Tat and I were chuckling about all this gamesmanship and wondering how it was going to come out. At about 11 PM, the phone rang one more time. This time it was Bill McKechnie. He said, "Bill, we'd like to have you. Fly down and visit with us. I'm sure we can work something out and make you happy." I said, "The only thing that will make me happy is for that $1,500 to be added to my contract." "Well," he said, "I don't know if we can do that. I'll have to talk to Warren." A little later Warren Giles rang again. "Can you be here by Sunday morning, ready to play?" he asked. "Yes, I can be there, ready to play." He sighed, "Come on down and we'll put the $1,500 in your contract." I said, "Thank you very much. I'm happy to be a Cincinnati Red."

So ended the cat and mouse game. I got myself down to Tampa lickety-split and played seven innings against the Boston Braves the day after I arrived. The club broke camp the next day and started on the trip north, playing the Red Sox and Ted Williams along the way.

The sale worked out extremely well for me. I had a good season in 1939, leading off, hitting .289, and leading the league in runs scored with 115. More important, we won Cincinnati's first pennant in twenty years, beating the St. Louis Cardinals by 4-1/2 games. It was a lot more fun playing on a pennant winner than struggling with Mr. Mack's tail-end clubs.

Near the end of the season when we had clinched the pennant and had just a couple of games to go, Mr. Giles asked me to come by his office because he wanted to see if we could work out a contract for 1940 before the World Series started. So I went in to visit Mr. Giles and he asked, "What do you want to play for us next year?"

"Mr. Giles," I said, "I really haven't given it a great deal of thought. But you know what I'm worth. Why don't you make me a reasonable offer?"

After he called, Tat and I had discussed what I should try to get and I had made up my mind what I wanted. When Mr. Giles named his figure, I said, "Mr. Giles, to be honest with you that is $1,500 more than I meant to get out of you. You were pretty decent last year in putting $1,500 into my contract, so I'm going to give you the $1,500 back." And, believe it or not, he took it.

I intended to retire from baseball after the 1940 season. My toe continued to plague me and cause problems with my legs, and the games were more work than pleasure. We won the Series in 1940, though. I knew another raise would be forthcoming, and I thought prospects for a third pennant were excellent, so I decided to play one more year.

In retrospect, the decision was probably not a good one. A harbinger of things to come occurred in Havana in March, where we had traveled to play three exhibition games against the Red Sox. One afternoon Frank McCormick, the 1940 National League MVP, decided to attempt a one and a half gainer in the hotel pool. He wrenched his back and played all year with a back brace. Although he never complained, he could not perform at his 1940 level.

We had a disappointing year, finishing third behind the Dodgers and Cardinals, twelve games out of first place. I had a tough time physically and could only start 107 games at third. So, after the season, I let Warren Giles know that I was retiring from baseball.

One afternoon in January, 1942, I was hard at work at the Werber Insurance Agency offices in the National Press Building in Washington when Mr. Giles called. The Reds, of course, still owned my contract. "Bill," he began, "the Chicago Cubs, Pittsburgh Pirates, and New York Giants are all interested in having you play for them this coming season. If you will go and play for one of them, I'll give you ten percent of the purchase price."

"What would you sell me for, Mr. Giles?" I asked.

He said, "The price is $35,000."

One does not have to be too bright to understand that ten percent of $35,000 is $3,500. I mulled that over and thought a $3,500 bonus up front was worth one more effort to play.

I said, "Sell me to the Giants."

"Bill," he asked, "if I send you the $3,500 and you change your mind about playing, will you send the money back to me?" I said I would and Mr. Giles said, "I'll put the check in the mail," and he did.

My 1942 season with the Giants was a decent enough ending. We had a good ball club, with Harry Danning, Johnny Mize, Bill Jurges, Dick Bartell, Joe Moore, Carl Hubbell, Hal Schumacher, Ace Adams, and player-manager Mel Ott, but we did not have the horses to beat the Cardinals or the Dodgers. We finished third, twenty games back, but did manage to come in ahead of my old Reds, who ended up fourth.

With about two weeks left in the season my toe became so painful that I told manager Ott I wanted to retire and leave the club immediately. I had already had a spell in Presbyterian Hospital in New York and my toe was hurting more and more. After discussions with Ott and owner Horace Stoneham, I put a few personal belongings in a small bag, said goodbye to the Polo Grounds, and headed for home and the world of business. I'd had a lot of fun in spite of my aching toe, and I'd gotten well paid for it.

World War II was on in full force, of course, and the following January I received a phone call from Clark Griffith. "Bill," he began, "You are aware that I've lost Buddy Lewis, my third baseman, to the Army Air Corps?"

"Yes, Mr. Griffith. I read about it in the *Post*."

"Well, Bill," he continued, "I want you to come to spring training with us and play third base for the Senators this year."

"Mr. Griffith," I said, "I can't do that because I'm on the list of voluntarily retired players and can't be reinstated to active status until ninety days after the start of the season."

"Oh, to hell with that," he replied, "I'll get that straightened out. You don't need to worry about that."

I said, "I can't do it, Mr. Griffith."

He said, "You've got to do it. I need a third baseman. I'll pay you more money than you've ever made in baseball."

"Mr. Griffith," I said, "if I played ball for you this summer, it would cost me thousands of dollars."

There was a long pause on the other end of the phone as that sunk in, and then Mr. Griffith spoke again. "Bill, you're either a damn big liar or you're making a helluva lot of money."

After the hassles I'd had about salary, I guess there is some irony in my turning down more money than I ever made in baseball before. But I knew that because of the pain in my big toe my baseball life would be limited, and I had worked diligently to prepare myself for a productive life when I could no longer hit, run, and field for a living. I did not play for the Senators in 1943, but I did place almost $2 million of life insurance with New England Life my first year out of baseball.

The following January, 1944, I was invited to hear Mr. Griffith speak at the weekly Cosmopolitan Club luncheon at the Hotel Washington. The war was still on, of course. We arrived early and sat at a table immediately in front of the speaker's lectern. Mr. Griffith spotted me and when he was introduced to speak he leaned over the head table, shook his long bony finger in my face, and said, "As for you, Bill Werber, last year I offered you a substantial salary to play ball for me and you wouldn't do it. This year you've got to come and play ball for me and I'm not going to pay you a damn thing. It's your patriotic duty." The crowd had a good laugh at my expense, but I was really and finally retired from baseball, so I laughed along with everyone else.

20 A LITTLE RUN-IN WITH THE COMMISSIONER

No story of baseball in the 1930s and 1940s could be complete without mention of Commissioner Kenesaw Mountain Landis. He ruled baseball with an iron hand and an iron will for twenty-five years. I had my audience with the Judge, but ironically only when I tried to retire from baseball. Although he ultimately treated me well, he let me know in no uncertain terms who was in control of the process.

Judge Landis was appointed to the federal bench in Chicago in 1905 by President Theodore Roosevelt. He gained public notoriety quickly in January, 1907, by fining Standard Oil of New Jersey a cool $29,240,000 in a freight rebate case, by far the largest fine ever inflicted on a corporate defendant. The fact that the Seventh Circuit Court of Appeals overturned the fine and ordered a new trial, in the process excoriating Landis for abusing his judicial discretion, was largely lost on the public.

A decade later, the upstart Federal League sued the American and National Leagues in his court, charging them with conspiring to monopolize baseball in violation of the antitrust laws. The Federal League had organized in 1913, and successfully raided the existing leagues of such star players as Eddie Plank, Chief Bender, Joe Tinker, Mordecai (Three Finger) Brown, Ed Reulbach, Lee Magee, and Hooks Wiltse. Organized baseball replied in kind and did all it could to repel the challenge of the upstart league. For example, the great Walter Johnson was wooed and signed by the new league, only to renege when Clark Griffith convinced the other American League owners to collectively pay a salary increase to Johnson for the good of the league.

The Feds chose Landis because of his hard line against monopolists, and because he was a devoted baseball fan. The judge, however, was reluctant to rule in the case, fearing that a judgment against Organized Baseball could destroy the game. During the ensuing delay the Federal League went down the tubes financially, rendering any type of injunctive relief moot. Five years later, when the baseball magnates needed a strong, sympathetic figure to clean up the game in the wake of the 1919 Black Sox Scandal, they selected Landis and gave him unprecedented powers to act "in the best interests of the game."

Public confidence in baseball was at an all-time low when Landis took office, and he quickly set about restoring it, suspending and banishing players right and left who were involved with gamblers. He suspended the eight White Sox players who were accused of throwing the 1919 World Series pending their trial, then banished them even though they were all acquitted by a Chicago jury. Thus began his reign as baseball's czar.

Landis never shied from controversy and ruled the game with an iron hand—sometimes arbitrarily. We as players knew that the Judge frowned on trips to the racetrack, although that never deterred some, as well as any fraternization with gamblers, or even opposing ballplayers. Gabby Hartnett, for example, incurred the Judge's wrath by posing in uniform for a picture with Chicago mobster Al Capone.

My own encounter with the Commissioner occurred in January, 1943, as a result of my retiring from the Giants. I had asked permission to leave the team because of the pain in my troublesome right toe, and said that I would relinquish my salary for the balance of the season and pay my own hospital expenses.

Manager Mel Ott said he had no objection, nor did Horace Stoneham, who was most cordial, willingly agreeing to my voluntary retirement. Later while I was cleaning out my locker in the clubhouse, Bill Terry, general manager of the Giants (and Hall of Fame first baseman), happened by and asked what I was up to. I told him, and we parted amicably.

Judge Landis. a no nonsense commissioner.

All was well until a day or two later, when a New York newspaper reported that I had left the Giants without permission and had been suspended by the club. If the club had suspended me rather than letting me retire, I wanted my two weeks salary and hospital expenses. I hastily dashed off a letter to Judge Landis asking for his help. I did not hear from Landis, so after a few weeks I wrote him a second time, asking rather casually if anything was being done in my interest. Still no response, so after two or three weeks I wrote again, suggesting that my previous two letters might have gotten lost.

Eventually, in January 1943, I got a call from Leslie O'Connor, secretary to the Commissioner, asking if it would be convenient for me to meet with the Judge the following Tuesday at 10 in the morning at his apartment in Chicago.

I looked forward to the meeting with trepidation. I knew Landis was a tough old coot, befitting his public image of a tousled head of white hair, a cold stare, and a sour grimace. Yet I also knew of his reputation as a man of courtesy and even grim humor, as a well-known story of a visit to the Lyric Opera in Chicago with Mrs. Landis suggests. It was an evening of fierce cold and ice underfoot as the Landis limousine pulled up under the opera's porte-cochere. The Judge, in black tie, emerged and held the door open for Mrs. Landis. He was heard to say to her in a sonorous voice, "Be very careful, Mama, lest you slip and break your goddamned ass." With a wink to onlookers and Mama safely beside him, he entered the opera hall. (Landis had good reason to be solicitous of Mrs. Landis: she had once broken her arm at home by tripping over his golf clubs.)

I stepped off the train in Chicago's Union Station that January and it was so cold my nostril hairs froze immediately. I arrived at the Judge's apartment at five minutes to 10, as did Bill Terry and Mel Ott, and found it was not much warmer inside, in more ways than one.

Leslie O'Connor opened the door and bade us enter. There in a high-backed chair sat Landis, wrapped in blankets to his armpits. He needed them, too, for the apartment was frigid. Apparently, the Judge was trying to contribute to the war effort by conserving fuel. His greeting to me was equally frosty, at least compared to the warm welcome he gave to Ott and Terry, extending his hand, calling them by name and solicitously inquiring after the health of their wives. Then he peremptorily muttered, "Now gentlemen, sit down, and, dammit, let's get this sorry business over with."

I noticed that the Judge had a stack of correspondence and assorted documents four or five inches high on his blanket-covered lap, so I realized he had not been ignoring my correspondence. It made me feel none too comfortable about my three letters. He did not refer to these papers but from beneath his craggy eyebrows he fastened his gaze on Mel Ott and began his interrogation.

"Mr. Ott," he said, "were you of the opinion that Mr. Werber was malingering late in the season?"

"No sir, Judge," Ott replied, "I knew he had a bad right leg."

"Did he ask your permission to leave the ballclub?" Landis continued.

"Yes, sir, he did," Ott reported. "I asked him to check it out with Mr. Stoneham."

"Mr. Terry," the Judge asked, turning to Bill, "did Mr. Werber speak to Mr. Stoneham following his conversation with Mr. Ott?"

"Yes, sir, Judge Landis, he did," confirmed Terry.

"And Mr. Terry," the Commissioner continued, "did Mr. Stoneham agree with Mr. Werber that he would consent to his voluntary retirement?"

"Yes sir, Judge," Bill answered, "he told me that he did."

"Why then, Mr. Terry," came the obvious question, "was information provided the press that Mr. Werber had left the ballclub without permission and was thereby suspended?"

"Well, sir," Terry explained, "I felt Mr. Werber would want to play again after a winter's rest. I pointed out to Mr. Stoneham that if he was placed on the voluntary retired list, he could not be reinstated for play until 90 days after the opening of the season. If suspended, he could be reinstated by us at any time. We acted in what we felt was the best interest of Mr. Werber."

I was relieved to hear this, but my euphoria was short-lived. Judge Landis next fixed his piercing blue eyes on me.

"Well now, Mr. Werber," he said, pursing his lips and flipping a couple of pages of the correspondence, "I believe you exhibited some impatience with me in the handling of this matter, did you not?"

I thought my letters had been courteous, temperate, and even casual, but the Judge obviously thought differently. I knew better than to deny his allegation.

"Yes, sir, Judge Landis, I did," I acknowledged.

The old gentleman stiffened in his high-backed chair, stared me down and declared icily, "Well, now, that's just too goddamned bad. I don't know whether I'll do anything for you or not."

There was nothing for me to say, so I kept quiet, feeling a little like Standard Oil must have felt some thirty-five years earlier. I heard nothing for a couple of weeks, and, needless to say, I made no inquiry. Then I received a letter from the Commissioner, upholding my voluntary retirement and requiring the Giants to pay both my hospital expenses and my salary for the last two weeks of the season. His decision certainly made me feel considerably better about leaving baseball. It also confirmed to me that the game was in good, if firm and tough, hands with Judge Landis.

21 HAPPY CHANDLER AND THE HALL OF FAME

Baseball never had a better fan nor one with a more genuine love for the game than Albert "Happy" Chandler. In 1939 he was governor of Kentucky and could be found in a box seat along the third base line of Crosley Field in Cincinnati on most Sundays and holidays. The Reds won their first pennant in twenty years, and Happy was an energetic and vociferous rooter who became part of the Reds' winning attitude.

Happy was not much in evidence during the 1940 season because he had been elected to the United States Senate and was attending to his duties in Washington. When the World Series came around, however, and Cincinnati and Detroit hacked away at each other, he was back in his customary seat hollering his head off for the Reds to make it all the way. When we did, he was in our clubhouse after the seventh game, sharing in the victory celebration, slapping players on the back and hugging everyone he could reach. He did not stay long, however. He was accompanied by his physician and after the game they drove to Christ Hospital for an emergency appendectomy. He had been determined, through clenched teeth and flushed face, to see the Reds crowned world champions if he died in his box seat to do it.

The next time I saw Happy Chandler was in early 1945, during his term in the Senate. He was dining alone at Fan and Bill's, a popular steak house on Connecticut Avenue across from the Mayflower Hotel when I happened upon him. He invited me to join him and I did. That very morning the Washington *Post* had reported that Chandler might be selected to replace the recently deceased Kenesaw Mountain Landis as baseball's commissioner. He read the article but dismissed it as highly improbable.

"That is a job I'd love to have," he said, "but I do not think they will really consider me."

Only a day or two later the *Post* made it known that Senator Albert B. Chandler had been named baseball's second commissioner. He served for six years, from April 24, 1945 to July 15, 1951, when he was denied a second term by a single vote. Only one owner voted against him, but four abstained, costing him his job.

Chandler was probably ousted for two reasons. First, his role in initiating and helping place the players' pension on solid ground won him no favors from the owners. Chandler negotiated baseball's first television contract with NBC and ensured that much of its proceeds went to the pension fund. Second, the owners had voted 15-1 against integration at the 1947 winter meetings, and they did not appreciate his role in paving the way for Jackie Robinson to rise to the big leagues. Chandler had given Brooklyn's Branch Rickey his unequivocal support to bring Robinson to the majors, in effect rebuffing the other fifteen owners. Armed with the Commissioner's support, Rickey did just that, although he seldom stopped to credit Happy for his role in integrating the game.

I had no contact with Chandler until 1978, when I noticed a blurb in the paper that friends and family were honoring Happy on the occasion of his eightieth birthday at his home in Kentucky. I dropped him a note congratulating him on this latest achievement and wishing him well. I received back a warm letter thanking me and recalling me as his favorite third baseman.

After renewing contact with my old friend, it began to bother me that Happy had never been elected to Baseball's Hall of Fame. Landis had been elected in 1944, the year he died, and Happy's successor, Ford Frick, had been elected in 1970, five years after he retired from the job. Frick had served as National League president for seventeen years and then fourteen

Happy Chandler—he didn't exactly quit as the headline suggests.

more as commissioner without, in my opinion, any particular distinction.

It began to rankle me more and more each year when the Hall of Fame elections were announced and Chandler was not elected. Finally, in 1981 I wrote Ken Smith, then director emeritus of the Hall of Fame, to ask for the names and addresses of the members of the Veteran's Committee of the Hall of Fame since it was they who were passing over Chandler each year. I first wrote my old teammate and manager Joe Cronin, who was on the committee. Joe wrote back that he supported the election of Chandler and was working for it within the committee.

I also wrote Al Lopez, the old catcher and manager of considerable reputation, asking his assistance in rectifying the injustice. Al's response was not promising, reporting that Chandler had not received enough votes to stay on the ballot and pointing out that the owners did not like Chandler although most of the players did. I wrote back that the Hall of Fame belongs to baseball, pointing out that none of the owners had ever been to bat in a major league game and urging him to "get in there and scrap!"

Gabe Paul was also a Veteran's Committee member and he provided a new committee list and promised to promote Chandler at the next meeting. I then wrote the rest of the committee, noting Happy's multiple accomplishments and advancing the possibility that history might condemn them for their failure to recognize such merit and service to the game. Almost all replied, some with lukewarm sentiments. Birdie Tebbetts, a member of the 1940 Tigers that my Reds had defeated in the World Series, was the most negative, telling me that I was "indicting baseball. You accuse us of neglect. . . . you question our motives by saying we *exclude*, when our function, as I see it, is to *include*."

I struck paydirt, however, with Joe Reichler, the veteran Associated Press writer and noted baseball historian. Reichler told me that he had campaigned without success for Chandler's election for the last two years. He was not optimistic because Bob Addie, the veteran Washington baseball writer, had been a staunch Chandler supporter, but had recently died.

Reichler also pointed out that part of the problem lay with the system. The committee was limited to two electees a year, one or both of whom must be a former major league player. Executives often got short shrift because they competed against managers, umpires, and former Negro Leaguers.

My letter, however, seemed to reenergize Reichler to the task. He contacted the committee members himself and reported to Chandler, who reported to me, that fence sitters Roy Campanella and Buzzie Bavasi would vote for the former commissioner. Then, lo and behold, he let us know that he had persuaded even Birdie Tebbetts to support Happy.

The Veteran's Committee met in Tampa, Florida, on March 10, 1982 and by secret ballot elected two new members, Travis Jackson, the former Giant shortstop, and Happy Chandler. I had kept Chandler apprised of my efforts on his behalf, and after his election he wrote me a very gracious letter which said in part:

> "I am sure you know that my love and affection for you is unbounded. We could not have made this successful run for the Hall of Fame without your determined efforts in my behalf....
>
> "You will be interested to know, Billy Boy, that I was a Boy Scout in 1915; one of the first in the United States. I, too, learned the lesson—do a good turn daily. I am honored to have been your good turn."

Happy continued to be grateful for my modest efforts on his behalf and every year during the Hall of Fame induction time in Cooperstown he would send me a note expressing his gratitude. The following is typical and arrived about six years after his election:

> "As long as I am above ground I will feel deeply obligated to you for your kindness to me. Except for your monumental

contributions to our cause, I feel that I would not have been elected to the Baseball Hall of Fame. That, of course, has been one of my greatest honors of this lifetime."

He passed away on June 15, 1991, about a month before his ninety-third birthday. I am thankful that he had almost a decade on this good earth to enjoy his rightful place in the Baseball Hall of Fame.

WERBER, William Murray   BR, TR, 5' 10" 170 lbs.   B. June 20, 1908, Berwyn, MD

CAREER MAJOR LEAGUE STATISTICS

	G	AB	H	2B	3B	HR	R	RBI	BB	SO	SB	BA	SA	POSITION
1930 NY-A	4	14	4	0	0	0	5	2	3	1	0	.286	.286	SS-3, 3B-1
1933 NY/BOS-A*	111	427	110	30	6	3	64	39	33	39	15	.258	.377	SS-71, 3B-39, 2B-2
1934 BOS-A	152	623	200	41	10	11	129	67	77	37	**40**	.321	.472	3B-130, SS-22
1935 BOS-A	124	462	118	30	3	14	84	61	69	41	**29**	.255	.424	3B-123
1936 BOS-A†	145	535	147	29	6	10	89	67	89	37	23	.275	.407	3B-101, OF-45, 2B-1
1937 PHA-A	128	493	144	31	4	7	85	70	74	39	**35**	.292	.414	3B-125, OF-3
1938 PHA-A‡	134	499	129	22	7	11	92	69	93	37	19	.259	.397	3B-134
1939 CIN-N	147	599	173	35	5	5	**115**	57	91	46	15	.289	.389	3B-147
1940 CIN-N	143	584	162	35	5	12	105	48	68	40	16	.277	.416	3B-143
1941 CIN-N§	109	418	100	9	2	4	55	46	53	24	14	.239	.299	3B-107
1942 NY-N	98	370	76	9	2	1	51	13	51	22	9	.205	.249	3B-93
11 YEARS	1295	5024	1363	271	50	78	875	539	701	363	215	.271	.392	3B-1143, SS-96, OF-48, 2B-3

CAREER HIGHLIGHTS

Equaled major league record by hitting 4 doubles in a game July 17, 1935. Led league in runs scored, 1939; stolen bases, 1934 and 1935, tied for lead in 1937. Scored five runs in a game July 6, 1934. First player to bat in a televised game, August 26, 1939. Led third basemen in fielding, 1940. Hit four successive doubles in 14-inning game, May 13, 1940, becoming first player to hit 4 doubles in a game in both leagues. Leading hitter in 1940 World Series.

* Sold to Boston Red Sox, May 12, 1933.
† Traded to Philadelphia Athletics for Pinky Higgins, December 9, 1936.
‡ Sold to Cincinnati Reds, March 16, 1939.
§ Sold to New York Giants, December 10, 1941.

WORLD SERIES STATISTICS

	G	AB	R	H	2B	3B	HR	RBI	BB	SO	SB	BA	SA	POSITION
1939 CIN-N	4	16	1	4	0	0	0	2	---	---	---	.250	---	3B-4
1940 CIN-N	7	27	5	10	4	0	0	2	---	---	---	.370	---	3B-7
TOTALS	11	43	6	14	4	0	0	4	---	---	---	.319	---	3B-11

CAREER MINOR LEAGUE STATISTICS

	G	AB	R	H	2B	3B	HR	RBI	BB	SB	BA	SA	POSITION
1930 ALBANY (EASTERN)	84	316	80	107	14	7	4	39	---	---	.339	---	ss
1931 TOLEDO (A.A.)	58	221	34	61	4	4	4	19	---	---	.276	---	3B, ss
1931 NEWARK (INT.)	52	142	22	30	3	0	0	6	---	---	.211	---	ss
1932 BUFFALO (INT.)	117	422	75	122	16	7	17	62	---	---	.289	---	ss
4 YEARS	321	1101	211	320	37	25	25	126	---	---	.291	---	3B, ss

AFTERWORD

Paul Rogers called on the phone this morning and advised me that our publisher, after reading the manuscript, thought we needed one more chapter to tie the book together. Paul is a law professor and former dean of the Law School at Southern Methodist University. It was he who prompted me to write this book and throughout he has been my collaborator, organizing and adding some here and there and subtracting where called for.

At the beginning I told him that I did not think the book needed anything about me in it. Paul pointed out to me that since the book was about baseball in the 1930s from my perspective, it was inevitable that I would be in it. I asked him to minimize me to the extent possible. I do not like self-serving people and, besides, the little I've accomplished in life has never impressed me. The mistakes I've made and how I worked to correct them, however, might be of value to someone. Hence, this final chapter. I was born in Berwyn, Maryland, on June 20, 1908, so I will turn ninety-three during 2001. Berwyn was a country town, about ten miles out of the District of Columbia. There wasn't a paved road in it, so it took great leg power to ride a bicycle. It had a feed store, a small grocery store and post office, and a barber shop, and not much else. Berwyn is no more. It's been absorbed and is now within the corporate limits of College Park, home of the University of Maryland.

To the east of Berwyn ran a small stream, Indian Creek, through some woods and swampland, and to the west about a half a mile ran another,

Paint Branch. We swam in those creeks during the summer and hunted water moccasins and stone rollers. In the winter time my older brother Fritz, my senior by four years, ran trap lines for muskrat and mink. We'd get up in the cold and dark of 4 AM to check out a section of stream where he'd set traps and head for home, sometimes with a muskrat or mink. If lucky, we'd skin the "rat," invert the skin, scrape the fat off, and hang it in the woodshed to dry. We then entered our home, changed our clothes, ate our breakfast, and caught the streetcar to school in Washington, D.C. A hardship? No. It was a lot of fun. Periodically, we sent the skins off to Topeka, Kansas, and the return of $8, $9, or $10 seemed like a fortune.

That is not to say that the Werbers were poor. My father left his employment with the Northwestern Mutual Life Insurance Company in June, 1904, and started his own business, the Werber Insurance Agency. He did well, but he held the opinion that his two sons should work for what they wanted. We had bikes and in season had footballs, basketballs, baseballs and bats, and even ice skates. In turn, we spaded and fertilized a large area in our backyard for the planting of corn, lima beans, peas, string beans, lettuce, radishes, cucumbers, tomatoes, and potatoes. When the potato vines flourished, about a million bugs appeared on the leaves, which we had to pick and put into Mason jars as proof positive that we'd done the job. We kept the wood box filled in the kitchen and when asked we cut off a chicken's head with a sharp hatchet and watched our mother fry it for dinner. There were always chores to do and we did them.

I graduated from the Langdon public school in Washington, D.C., in the early summer of 1922 and entered Tech High School in September of that year. My Dad did not have a high opinion of the schools in Prince Georges County, Maryland. He did want me to join the cadets and work my way up in four years to become colonel of the Cadet Corps. He bought me a gray uniform with hat and after school I stood erect at shoulder arms and moved in unison upon shouted directions. I didn't like it. I didn't like regimentation, and when in the spring it began to get warm and the bulletin board called for tryouts for baseball, I said to hell with it. Unbeknownst to my father, I began to spend my afternoons playing baseball at the Washington Barracks since Tech had no practice field of its own. I can't recall exactly when he discovered the deception, but I do remember the alienation it caused. I can't even remember making the team and, therefore, I guess I didn't.

About this time, I got my priorities all screwed up. I wanted to make All High in basketball and my studies seemed insignificant by comparison. It wasn't that I was dumb. I was an Eagle Scout with thirty-six merit badges and one of them was in *bee keeping*. You had to build a hive, make the cover, attract the bees and then market the honey. I made All High in basketball and baseball for three years but neglected my school work. I faced the dire prospect of not being able to graduate with my class in June, 1926, an embarrassment to me, to my family, and to the girl with whom I had fallen in love.

My section teacher, Mrs. Eda B. Frost, came to my rescue. She pleaded with the principal at Tech to permit me to go to classes all seven periods during the day and then return to night school for a class in algebra. It woke me up.

In September, 1926, I entered Duke University on a scholarship, awarded I hasten to add for proficiency in athletics and not academics. The scare at Tech High School prompted me to load up at Duke so that by my senior year I needed only one required course to graduate. I did well at basketball, making a number of All-American selections, and did even better at baseball, signing a contract with the New York Yankees after my freshman year to take effect upon graduation. Of greater satisfaction, and of more lasting benefit, was the Robert E. Lee Award, Duke's highest at the time to a graduating senior. As Dean William Hane Wannamaker shook my hand and presented me with my diploma, he added in a quiet voice, "William, I don't know of anyone I'd rather give this to." I'll never forget that one.

With four more-than-decent years at shortstop for Duke's baseball team, hitting around .400 each year, I had a pretty good opinion of myself. You might describe me as "cocky." As I viewed it, I possessed plenty of "self-confidence." In 1930, a large margin of difference between baseball at Duke and baseball with the New York Yankees existed and I learned quickly that I needed more experience. It was not until 1933 that I became the shortstop for the Boston Red Sox. In 1934, nearing the end of the season, in a fit of anger and petulance, I drop-kicked a water bucket full of ice in the Red Sox dugout and broke my right big toe. The toe required surgery but was never right. I played for eight more years in the major leagues, always in pain.

This act of stupidity taught me a lesson. During each winter thereafter I worked hard at selling insurance from my father's office. I had a wife and two children for whom to provide, and the fragile toe could abort my baseball earnings at any time. There was also the matter of a mortgage on a fine home that demanded attention. I retired from the New York Giants in September, 1942, and voluntarily gave up a $13,500 salary—more than decent for the times, but tip money today. In 1943, working full-time at selling, I earned over $100,000, considerably more than paid to bank presidents or the heads of universities, and $20,000 more than Babe Ruth's best contract. In the thirty years of selling prior to retirement in January, 1972, I never made less.

Upon my retirement from baseball in 1942, the ladies at St. Andrews Episcopal Church in College Park, without my knowledge or permission, appointed me to revitalize the moribund Boy Scout Troop #228. They counted upon my dear wife Tat to deliver the news of my selection. She did and I did, for about three years.

From Scoutmaster, I was asked to serve as commissioner for scouting for Prince Georges County with a population of some 700,000 and a large number of scout troops. After a stint at that job, I was tagged as camping chairman for the National Capital Area Council, second to Detroit as the largest in America. We had six camping sites that had to be staffed and provisioned and made ready for use by the scouts in D.C. and the surrounding counties in Maryland and Virginia. Each camp had its own chairman and staff—all volunteers. I had that job for seven years.

Shortly thereafter the professional, paid scout leaders decided to put on a capital-funds campaign, the first in the long history of the National Capital Area Council. They asked me to chair it and I accepted. After all was said and done, the Council honored me with the Silver Beaver Award.

In 1946, I was complimented by my university. The Board of Trustees of Duke voted to establish a program of annual giving. The alumni secretary, Charles A. Dukes, came to my office in Washington and asked me to chair the effort. It runs to this day. In 1952, I was asked by Duke to serve as president of the Alumni Association and was pleased to accept. All three of my children are Duke graduates, Bill in '53, Patricia in '56, and Susie in '69. Bill was an All American in baseball in both '52 and '53.

Whatever I have accomplished can be attributed to my wife, Kathryn Potter Werber, who passed away March 11, 2000, at age ninety-one. We were married on September 16, 1926, and she returned with me to Duke and shepherded me through my senior year. We enjoyed over seventy years of marvelously happy life. She wanted to live long enough to read this book. I ache that she cannot.

Acknowledgments

Many good people selflessly supported and aided the writing of this book; Bo Carter, John Esch, Robin Roberts, Earl Weiskittel and especially Julie Patterson Forrester read all or part of the manuscript to its betterment. Mark Alvarez was helpful in many ways, not the least of which was his skilled editing. A.W. Suehsdorf's copy editing helped the final product as well. Bill Bozman and Ronnie Joyner donated their considerable talents for the cover design, as did Glenn LeDoux for the layout. Norman Macht believed in and supported the project from the first time he learned of it. Bill Werber, Jr. was continually helpful and I'll never forget the wonderful hospitality of my co-author Bill Werber, Sr. and his wife Tat during my visit with them. Bill promised a visit with Ted Williams when I visited and did he ever deliver. Greg Ivy was his normal efficient self in aiding with resource materials and Sharon Magill was ever cheerful in administrative support. Thanks also to Talmage Boston who first put me in touch with my future co-author. Little did anyone know that this book would result.

C. Paul Rogers III
February 2001

INDEX